CONSEQUENCES
Short Stories • Poems • Commentaries

RON IANNONE

Destination Press
Morgantown, West Virginia

ISBN: 978-0998202006

I am grateful to Joyce Akers for letting me use materials from her diaries in "Skaneateles." The excerpts are italicized.

For my children, Mary Beth, Jeff, and Patrick
&
my grandchildren, Megan, Justin, Joey, and Sonny
&
my great-grandchild, Mason.

Contents

Preface

Over several years ago I started to make observations and would write them on index cards. I then would throw them into a drawer of a file cabinet. All kinds of stuff I would write about. Usually, I would write in between classes, just before going to bed or early in the morning. These index cards had everything from poems to ideas for stories to descriptions of fall leaves, piles of snow, the deep penetrating eyes of a friend, and relationships. I had over 2,000 index cards, and included here are just a small sample from, or inspired by, these cards.

I
SHORT STORIES

The Shooter

She's yelling again from downstairs to hurry up or we're going to be late for school. I don't fucking care about school. Soon there will be no school for me and a lot of other people. However, I like the same schedule every morning: Get up at 6:16, shower at 6:18, get dressed at 6:30 in my navy blue shirt. I have thirty of them, and also I wear navy blue Dockers pants along with a black t-shirt. I have forty of them except for one white shirt I wear for funerals and formal occasions. At 6:45 I take the Adderall so I can concentrate somewhat and don't go wild like yesterday at the grocery where I pushed all of the Hunts tomato sauce cans off the shelves. We left the grocery store quickly. Order was back when I came home and buried myself under the thick comforter on my bed. My mother didn't say anything.

"OK, OK, I'm coming!" I yell as I go downstairs so she will stop fucking yelling for me to come down. Before I leave my room I make sure I fold my navy blue washcloth and navy blue towel into perfect squares. Both are hanging on the towel rack with the washcloth first and the towel to the left.

On the way down I also hit my right pocket to make sure my light-blue rosary beads are in there along with a perfectly folded white handkerchief on top. I am forgetting to mention that before I leave my room I check my closet in order to open a large black gun case that holds a TEC-DC 9M pistol and a 9 mm Hi-Point 995 Carbine. I rub them both for luck before I leave. Tonight, I think, I need to sneak out again when she's asleep to see my stuff in the storage unit. My mother knows

3

about the guns in the closet but doesn't know about the storage unit ones.

Once downstairs, I grab a bowl for my Fruit Loops, taking every color out except for the little blue pieces. Then, before I go out the door, I wipe the doorknob with a Kleenex. My mom follows. She works mostly at home for Gold Printing. She's a graphic artist. She tried to homeschool me for a couple of years, but the doctor thought it may be good for me to go to school so I can learn how to interact socially. I hate interacting with assholes. Gold Central High School is full of them. All of them there think I am a freak and a weirdo. I see when we arrive that mostly everyone is inside the school. The rectangular red brick building reminds me of a prison without bars. I grab my backpack from the backseat. My mother leans to give me a kiss on the cheek. I let her, but I won't let anyone else because I hate to be touched. Sometimes a teacher will touch me as a friendly gesture, and I will flinch as if I were given an electric shock.

"Bye," she says. "I'll be here at 2:45 to pick you up."

"Okay."

Before I open the doors to the school, I take out my white handkerchief and wipe down the huge, brass, curved door-knob. Quickly, with my head down, I go to my locker and place all of my books inside except for what I need for English Composition and Advanced College Math. I place them in my backpack and hurry toward my math class. I look inside the window of the door and see almost everyone is there. Angelina, an overweight girl, pushes ahead of me and opens the door and I follow. Thank God, I think, I won't have to wipe the doorknob down. I head to the back and take a seat. Everyone looks at the freak as I sit. Mr. Walters is a fat-cheeked teacher, sloppily dressed in a red checked flannel shirt with wrinkled khaki pants. He is talking about binomials and factoring. I know this stuff. I hate it when we repeat stuff we've done over and over in previous math classes. Shit, if I had one of my guns now I would blast all of them, even Alice, whom I would like to get to know. She's a skinny redhead with a warm smile. Every day she tries to talk to me, but I put my head down and walk away except when she asks me if I like the musical group Maroon 5. I say yes and talk until the bell rings and we both go to the next class. No one else will talk to me because I'm the kid with autism or, more specifically, Asperger's. I wonder what they would think if they knew I was into school killings. I can't get enough of Eric Harris and how he planned the Columbine killings. In a way, as I read about Adam Larzo killing all those little kids in Connecticut, I see myself somewhat like him, but I would never kill little kids. Big kids are for me, I think to myself, and laugh out loud as the other kids look at me strangely. Also I can't help but laugh my ass off when I see videos of the shit-faced, crazy-eyed guy with bright red hair who killed all those people in that Colorado theatre. Lately, the jihad killings in Paris and California interested me, but my jihad will be the best. The school counselor says I should develop other interests like sports. I don't think the jocks would like that because they all think I'm a fag. I'm slight of build, very thin, pimple-faced, with an odd-shaped head and curly black hair. I'm not really ugly but I'm not really good-looking. I'm one that could easily fade into the crowd and no one would miss me. My mother says I've got to make friends. She wants to invite kids my age over and I tell her if she does I will run away and never come back. I know she doesn't understand why I like guns so much, but she says it's okay that they are in the house with her being a single woman and all of that. She even goes with me to target practice. Thank God she never goes to the storage unit with me because I then think she would think there was something wrong with me. The guns I have in the house came from mail order, but the ones in the storage unit all came from the streets.

At noon I eat my lunch outside near a wooded area away from everyone. And when it's bad weather I go to the gym and sit up high on the bleachers to the left. I eat the same sandwich every day, turkey on wheat with very little mayo, and two Chips Ahoy chocolate chip cookies. I hate the school cafeteria because there are too many people, and I hate the noise of the jerks who bring their lunches in crumpling paper bags. Most of all, I hate those fluorescent lights and the high frequency sounds when they flicker. The classroom lights I also hate. Their noise is nothing like the fluorescent lights in the cafeteria. Usually I stay wherever I'm at lunch until I hear the bell for my history class. Sometimes I write in a small black notebook about the TV shows I love, like *Law & Order*, *Criminal Minds*, and *Dateline*. My notes are always on how the criminals accomplish the crimes. The writing in the notebook seems to calm me. Many of the thoughts are my manifesto just like Eric Harris. Also when I really get upset about something, I rub the rosary beads in my pocket over and over again, mumbling "Hail Mary, full of grace." We are Catholic and go to Sunday mass every so often. I love the bright colors of the vestments the priests wear. Sometimes the mass is sung in Latin. It makes me think of angels singing. Everything seems right with the world when I'm there. I learned the prayers for the mass when my mother sent me to Catholic school for the first two years of elementary school until she decided to homeschool me.

As I walk back to school, I think about what my mother said the other night. She said she had just read that Mozart, Einstein, Warhol, Jane Austen, and even Thomas Jefferson all had Asperger's. I doubt that very much. Did they go crazy and break all of the windows at St. Mary's like I did in a violent rage? That's really why Mother homeschooled me. They kicked me out.

For the rest of the day, I go to classes but in a sense I am situationally retired. I'm there physically but mentally thinking of the big day coming soon. I can't wait to see those scared faces and helpless looks of the students, especially because we are considered one of the best high schools in central New York. Right now, I just don't know if I need all those pipe bombs I have. There is so much more planning I have to do before tomorrow, even though I have been planning the shootings for months.

As I leave school and head to where my mom is parked, no one speaks to me, just like any other day. Soon these stupid people, especially the rich kids, will wish they had spoken to me. I'm invisible to them. Basically, I don't care. I live in my head most of the time, so when people speak to me, I see their lips moving but I don't hear. Right now, my focus is planning the demise of the school. Eric Harris was a god, like I will be. For once in my life I'll have power and control. I now open the car door and get in.

"Hi," my mother says.

"Hi," I say.

"How was school?" she asks.

"The same."

"Do you mind? I have to stop and get some groceries."

"Fine. I won't go in because—."

"I know."

As I wait in the parking lot of Wegmans, I think about how I used to have a friend. Her name was Jenny but she moved away in the eighth grade. That's the last and only friend I had. I thought someday I could work something up with her but I could never have a sexual experience with anyone because of the touching thing. But I liked walking in the woods with Jenny and talking about deep thoughts such as: Is there a God? What happens to us when we die? We both felt nothing happens to us except being piles of leftover atoms, neutrons, and electrons. Our discussions were far ahead of what we talked about in school. Sometimes I did try talking to other kids about these topics. They would look at me and say, "You're weird." So I am, and they will see how weird I am tomorrow. All these assholes just want to talk about who is going out with whom after the football game. My mother says I don't try to make friends, but I do, and time after time they reject me.

So every day I follow the schedule; however, when the day is chaotic or there is too much noise in my head, I just sit at my desk, touch the rosary beads and repeat over and over, "Hail Mary, full of grace. Hail Mary, full of grace." But when there are too many conversations in the hall before class, I freak out. Also the noises in the cafeteria when everyone is talking at the same time drive me crazy. Sometimes I look forward to going to class because it's only one teacher talking. I especially like it when the teacher just lectures and doesn't interact with students. If it gets too bad in the hall, I wear earplugs. I tried wearing earphones with them turned off, but my mother said I looked stupid.

After we get back from the store, I help by carrying in the groceries and then tell her I have some homework to do in my room. I lie. I am really going to plan to wipe everyone out tomorrow. Tonight I need to sneak out at nine, after my mom goes to bed. She never hears me because she's a solid sleeper for at least four hours. The storage unit is about a mile away. She never goes there, so everything stored there is safe. Sometimes when I'm having a wild day, I go there to space out on the old furniture my parents had before they divorced. I was eleven. I don't remember my dad very much except he worked a lot and would play catch with me and then he was gone. My mother says he found someone better than her. That's it. And so it goes.

I know she is hurting, but I don't always understand her body language. That's quite normal for someone with Asperger's. It is pointless to expect me to look at her and know how she is feeling simply because her smile is too tight and she is hunched over and hugging her arms to herself, just as it would be pointless to expect a deaf person to hear a voice.

My mother is always complaining that I have no interests. But I do. I like my guns, and I like it when we go together to the shooting range. She thinks it's good that she learns how to shoot in case someone breaks into our house. I know she would go bullshit if she knew I had all the stuff at the storage unit.

8

I think I will wear the duster with a black turtleneck, pants, shoes, and even underwear, all black. I want to look good when they carry me away.

I am going to place the bombs in the bathrooms and then set them up by a timer. I also think, it is April and that's when Columbine, Oklahoma City bombing, and the Boston bombing took place. I think I've learned a lot about hychrozine, perchlorate, and nitroglycerin. The Internet has been great in teaching me about elements for bomb making. I'm not sure how many knives to bring, though.

I hope they find my manifesto like they did after my hero Eric did his thing at Columbine. I think it's small enough that it will fit in the rear between my back and belt. After I get back from the storage unit, I will hide under the bed with the thick comforter. I love the security. Today I thought how opposites, like hell being opposite of heaven, are true. That the devil is really God. I must put that in my manifesto. I also must put in that killing is good because that's the devil's work. If he is God that it's good. Anyway, after I hear my mother go to bed I wait an hour and quietly go down the stairs and go out the front door. It only takes me ten minutes to arrive at the storage unit. Except for a few street lights, it is nearly all black. I take out my flashlight and quickly open the padlock. Once inside, I shine the light on an assortment of boxes and containers that I worked on this past year. There are also roof cement, about four Styrofoam coolers, a box of ammunition, three pipe bombs, two camouflage bags, three pressure cookers, a SKS assault rifle with sixty rounds of ammunition, a Beretta 9 mm handgun, and a .22 caliber rifle. I know I am not going to use all of them for tomorrow's shootings. But I know I was going to use the .22 on my mother. I place the Beretta and .22 caliber rifles along with the pipe bombs in the bags.

I go home, drop off the .22 rifle and take a handgun and a rifle out of the closet and then leave for the school. Carrying the camouflage bag, I head for the side door of the gym which

I know will be open because the jocks use it sometimes late at night for practice. I hope I see them tomorrow because it will be "Hasta la vista, Baby" for them. Stupid jerks! I still don't get the basketball game of putting a ball in a basket. I place the bag under the bleachers and I know I'll be there early in the morning to get them. I take the pipe bombs out then slip the bags underneath the bleachers again. Now I run to the first floor bathrooms and place the bombs in the stalls with their timers set for 7:15 a.m. My plan is to get there around 6:30 a.m. School opens at 6:00 a.m. As I leave, I decide I'm glad I brought the shotgun because I can't wait to shoot someone in the head and then see blood and muscles splattered all over. Mr. Walters will be the first to go. I will shoot him in his beer gut and watch him gurgle blood and phlegm. He is so stupid, like most of the teachers, except for Mrs. Cronin, my English teacher. I love her interpretations of poems, but she has to die. All of them have to die. Also I can't wait to shoot out all the fluorescent lights. As I said, their noise drives me crazy. Really I love darkness and the numbers *9*, *99*, and *999*. I also love the letters *w* and *x*. I don't know why. I just do.

I hurry back home because it is getting near eleven, and sometimes my mother gets up at eleven and checks on me. If I'm on the computer, she tells me to go back to bed. My mom will get up at 4:30 a.m. tomorrow because she has to go in to work. She likes to pretty herself up before she leaves at 5:45 so she can drop me off at 6:00 a.m. But today she won't make it because I will be driving. I love driving, but she doesn't let me drive by myself because she thinks I will have an Asperger's episode.

I get up at 4:00 a.m., get dressed, and head toward my mom's room. She is in the bathroom. I have the .22 caliber rifle loaded. Quietly, I open her bathroom door and see through the frosted glass that she is in the shower. Opening the shower door, I say, "Good morning, Mom." She screams with a "please don't" on her fearful face. I shoot her nine times so that the shower has more blood than water. "Good-bye, Mommy Dearest."

Downstairs, I take the car keys from the magnetic hook on the refrigerator. I throw the rifle in the backseat. The school parking lot is almost empty. I park the car near the woods, and I lay the keys inside. The side entrance to the gym is still open as I move toward the bag underneath the bleachers. Grabbing the bags now, I head toward the library, passing some teachers. None of them know me because there are over 2,000 students. So I just smile as I pass. I can see more students are coming in and heading toward their lockers. Soon they will know me and the whole world will know me.

Once I get to the library, I set the bag down and take out a 9 mm Hi-Point 995 Carbine shotgun. Once loaded, I begin shooting at the few students in the library and at the two librarians who quickly duck behind the counter. Some students try to run, but I shoot them and yell, "May the Lord bless you." I ask one student if he believes in God. He says, "Yes." "Too bad," I say. "The devil is my God." I use a pistol on him. Still, for some reason, I don't know why the bombs are not going off. I run to the classroom next door to the library and open the door and shoot Mr. Lourdes, the civics teacher, and all the students that are in there. I hope I break the record for school killings. I think: Eric, I'm coming home. As I run toward the entrance, I shoot at students who are frozen in front of their lockers. At the entrance I turn and take the pistol out of my belt, place it to my temple, and pull the trigger.

Headline in the *Gold Herald* the next day reads: "School Shooter Kills Himself and 35 Students and Faculty. A New Record!"

The Private School Murder

I was involved in murdering my friend in 1958. There were four of us who did it. No one suspected us. We were the bright leaders of a private military school we attended near Syracuse, New York. We were seniors at Greenwood Military, where most of the class had been accepted into West Point, U.S. Naval Academy, and top ivy schools.

Today, the three of us still living are in our seventies and retired, having been successful in our careers. For the first time, we will all be together for our 50th reunion, except for Freddy. None of us have ever talked about what we did to Aaron in the early spring of 1958. I have thought about Aaron every day since it happened. I often wondered if Mr. Darling, our English teacher, ever suspected us. The four of us took an honors course in American literature from him.

Since retirement, the memory of that night causes me to break out in cold sweats, tremble terribly, and feel like I am burning up with a high fever. My doctor says I am having panic attacks. He prescribed Ativan, which I now take three or four times a day. Some days when I shake so bad inside I take five or six Ativan. I am addicted to them and no one knows, not even my wife, Sally. I couldn't live without them daily. I think once we get together at the reunion we can find a way to bring up Aaron so that it is out in the open. I thought the memory would fade, but it hasn't. Now I am haunted by the memory of Aaron's frightened face as he gasped for air and then went limp like a caught fish squirming all over the ground until one steps on it harder and harder until it stops. It's all a haze now, choking him first, then Freddy shooting him in the forehead. Then we took turns shooting him, I think. Even though I fought in Vietnam and killed several Viet Congs, those killings never bothered me because they were the enemy and they were killing my buddies. But what we did to Aaron that night is forever on my mind.

It was easier to block out that night when I was younger and working for G.E. designing jet engines in Liverpool, New York. Presently, just living with Sally, and my three children gone, pursuing their careers throughout the United States, I have discovered I have too much time to think. We travel throughout the United States and Europe and I golf three times a week with my retired friends. I live in Virginia Beach where the sea helps calm my nerves. Still, there is Aaron's face staring up at me as we threw dirt and leaves on his body. The one thing about being in Vietnam was I thought if I got killed there I would be free of Aaron's scared face. He fought as he was being choked by Freddy. I still don't understand why then we had to take turns shooting him. He scratched the shit out of Freddy's face so that blood was scattered all over Freddy's clothes. In fact, all of us got blood on us. Freddy was overweight and had a small, round face with eyes you could hardly see.

I am tall and lanky and always thought I looked like a tall Al Pacino with blond hair. Recently, I saw some photos of Jim and Henry on Facebook. They still look like they did at Greenwood. Jim is bulkier with thinning sandy hair and Henry looks great; the years of jogging and lifting seemed to have paid off. He now has a beautiful set of teeth that must've cost him thousands of dollars. Anyway, as I drive with my wife to Greenwood on Interstate 81, I think about how much I love central New York with its beautiful Finger Lakes amidst rolling lush green hills, especially in the summer. Many of the small towns like Skaneateles are perfect postcard settings. Suddenly, I think about Freddy who died just before our graduation. Everyone said it was suicide. His body was discovered at the bottom of Fall Creek Falls near Cornell. There is a gorge nearby made up of rock, water, and trees. You can get to the gorge from Linn Street in downtown Ithaca. We had all been there several times to drink beer, vodka, and picnic with girls from the nearby girls' school, Cazenovia College. The police said there was evidence on the way down the 400-foot drop that he tried grasping for grass and small trees. I often wondered if someone pushed him because so many guys didn't like him. I sort of also felt sorry for him, which is why he was with us that night.

I met my wife at one of the dances Greenwood held so that we could meet the girls from Cazenovia College and perhaps eventually marry. Most of the boys at Greenwood came from well-to-do families, as was true of the girls from Cazenovia. Sally, who is a former Miss New York State, is in her sixties now and is still as beautiful. She has greyish hair mixed with chestnut curls, a milky complexion, and soulful brown eyes. She is a great companion and friend during these active retirement years.

When we arrive at the Greenwood campus, I become very nervous. We find the desk to register underneath an opensided tent. While we finish registering, I see Jim and Henry approaching. Soon we are all shaking hands and hugging. Both are impressed with Sally's beauty. On the way to the table assigned to our class of 1958, I find out that Jim has retired from U.S. Steel as Vice-President of Accounting. He is divorced, has two children who are doing well in Seattle, and now he has a girlfriend in the area. Also, he volunteers at Greenwood to help raise funds for the school. Henry is also divorced, with no children, and had run his father's publishing business called Lakeside Publishing, which specialized in murder mysteries. Quickly, I wonder if he has written about Aaron's murder under a fake name.

While we sit at our assigned table, Jim and Henry flirt with Sally. She loves it, and I don't mind because for a while it keeps our minds off the real reason we have come together. We drink beer and ale, eat clams and chicken, and try to listen to former alumni talk about how Greenwood changed their lives. Afterward, Jim takes us around the campus, which is old, worn, and tired-looking with buildings almost 100 years old. Jim makes Henry and me pledge $50,000 each for the building campaign. Later, we end up at the Washington Tavern where we used to go after school to grab shakes, hamburgers, hot dogs, and great fries. The chain restaurant Shake Sack is no better than the Tavern. Sally leaves us to go back to the hotel. She is tired from the drive from Virginia Beach. I kiss her good-bye. We head for a table in the rear and order more beers and the Tavern's favorite hamburger and fries. Alcohol is served on the reunion weekends. For a long moment no one says anything. Finally, Jim asks quietly, "Do any of you think of Aaron?"

I say, "Every day. Should we talk about it after all these years? We never did, and the police told his parents that he ran away to Europe like a lot of the rich kids did in the fifties and sixties."

"I got some information about Aaron's parents," Jim says.

"Good," I say.

"His parents just donated two million dollars to name the new theatre in his name."

"Good," I think. However, he never showed any interest in theatre. Hell, all he wanted to do was to go out.

"Remember," Henry says, "we used to write his love letters to his pimple-faced girlfriend, Lola. He just didn't have the vocabulary or the understanding of adjectives and adverbs. Mr. Darling worked his ass off trying to get him to understand when to use them."

"I know," I say. "What was his nationality?"

"Italian," Jim says.

"I felt sorry for him," I say. "Henry, you worked with him to speak in complex sentences."

"Yeah," Henry says. "He would get nervous and end up saying 'he neither was supposed to do it.' He would get his words backwards. Today, a speech pathologist would correct it in a few sessions."

For the next few hours we drink a lot of beer as we catch up with our lives until Jim brings up Aaron again.

"We got to do something about Aaron now."

"I agree," I say. Henry nods in agreement. I think about Aaron and how small he was with an angelic face with freckles across his nose. He didn't look Italian; he looked Irish. He had dark short hair with matching watery eyes.

"I wondered," I ask, "why his body was never found? And how the hell did it happen? I don't remember much of that night. Freddy said he was bringing the M-16 to shoot birds."

"All I know," Jim says, "Mr. Darling told us earlier in class that day how to free ourselves from the material world so the divine could enter our souls. I remember we fasted all day and only ate junk food. Then we drank gin and vodka. Remember he said St. Theresa of Ávila and St. John of the Cross fasted all the time so the divine lived in them. Greeks would have these celebrations where they fasted, and through meditation and prayer they moved into the spiritual and lost the material world."

"Hell," Jim continues, "Remember Darling talked about that Russian writer. What was his name, Oupsen? Oh, I know—Ouspensky."

"Darling was really into some weird stuff," Henry says.

"All I remember," I say, "was we were all drunk and laughing our asses off. Then Aaron started yelling 'I'm drunk, I'm fucking real fucking drunk.' Then all of us at once jumped him to be quiet. Then I remember now that Freddy started to choke him and then Aaron tried to scratch his eyes out as he fought for his life. And then Freddy getting up, grabbing the M-16, shooting him in the forehead. A little brownish hole appeared. Then we all took turns shooting him. I now think it was all part of the celebration to have the divine come into us. Then I remember everything got real quiet. All I heard were the crickets singing their nightly songs. Freddy ran off. Then we buried Aaron with some dirt and leaves and placed over him a long aluminum cylinder-shaped container that probably was used in the nearby heating plant for the school."

"I can't believe they never found him," Jim says.

"Right," Henry agrees. "I thought afterward we would get off on manslaughter charges."

I get up. "Let's see if we can find him. Remember it's directly in back of the Tavern here. I think."

We get up, go to the woods, and use our iPhones as flash-lights and after about thirty minutes we find the aluminum container. Quickly we move it and begin to dig underneath until Henry starts to yell, "Shit, I found his skull. Oh my God, his…Aaron's skull!" He holds it up and we shine our phones on it as if it is a treasure.

Jim screams. "Put it back!"

Henry obeys and both Jim and Henry begin burying the skull with leaves and dirt. All three of us replace the container back on Aaron's body.

On the way back to the Tavern, I ask, "Should we go to the Police?"

"No," Henry says. "Let it be or we will all be ruined. What do we have—four or five years left before we're hit with strokes, heart problems, Alzheimer's, dementia, or whatever."

"I agree," Jim says.

"I'll kill myself before I go to jail," Henry adds.

"I don't know if I can live with the guilt," I say.

"Fuck the guilt," Jim says. "I just want to live."

Jim drives me back to the hotel and just before I open the car door to leave, he leans over and touches my arm. "Forget it, my friend. If you need to talk, call, okay?"

"I'll see." I close the door and walk toward the entrance of the hotel. Still, I can see the blood, dripping from Aaron's lips. A few years ago Sally and I were in Bulgaria on a river cruise. I thought I saw Aaron in the distance, from an outside café we were eating at. He looked fit and happy. He was about the same age as when he died. I got up and walked in his direction and saw a small, burned hole in the middle of his forehead. He smiled at me and as I got closer, he vanished. For me, this was the end of the story and I thought that Aaron's smile was saying that I was forgiven and to move on to the rest of my life.

Perhaps, I thought, he now works for the CIA. Even though he had some problems with speech, he would be a prime candidate for he always wanted to know what was going on.

He was definitely a pain in the ass; however, his blood-splattered face and the brownish hole in the middle of his forehead will always be there. And I still don't know when Freddy handed the M-16 to me because I was so drunk and maybe the whole thing about the divine was all bullshit. I heard so many shots that night, and I am tired of living two lives, one of them being a good person who is well respected in the community and the other one who is evil and murderous. It has been literally driving me crazy every day since it happened. I can't transcend this evil in my life.

Someone seems to be calling me now as I turn toward the hotel's parking lot. Beyond I can see cars speeding by on the highway that is the overpass for Interstate 81. Once again, I hear someone calling me as I now head toward the wall that protects people from traffic. Once there, I stare down to the interstate and see the blue and red lights of two squad cars chasing a bright red Audi sports car. Enough is enough. I know that voice in my head is you, Aaron, and what a pain in the ass you still are, even in death. Listen, my friend, here is the truth: We deeply loved each other more than you could ever imagine, and that's why we had to get rid of you. Now full of anger, I quickly turned around and walked back to the hotel.

———⟨•⟩———

Respite

She was ninety-eight and would soon be ninety-nine years old. She was about eighty pounds with a frail body that at one time in the 1950s had men whistling as she walked by with her slim, swimsuit body. Then, she had curly light brown hair framing a beautiful moon-shaped face. I also remember her taking me shopping or meeting her in front of Edwards Department Store where she worked as a buyer. We lived in Seneca Falls, New York. It was a small hamlet near two of the most popular of the Finger Lakes: Seneca and Cayuga. Some say Seneca Falls was the inspiration for Frank Capra's "It's a Wonderful Life." It was also the home of the women's rights movement.

My mother, Maretta, sometimes would take me to Hunters Diner down the main street from Edwards. She would always buy me one of their famous chocolate milkshakes and a basket of their crispy fries with homemade ketchup. The diner looked like an old railroad dining car painted silver grey. It was small with ten stools at the counter and six booths. Once she didn't show up in front of the store and I got lost until a cop brought me home to an empty house. She never said a word about it afterward. I often wondered if she was trying to lose me because she frequently talked about never wanting to be married. She wanted to be a career woman and work at Saks off Fifth Avenue in New York.

There was something else about my mother that I think began then, and that was her Obsessive Compulsive Disorder. She was a clean freak. Everything had to be sparkling and dust free. I still remember foil on all stove and refrigerator handles. The hardwood and linoleum floors were waxed so much that when she wasn't around I would practice skating and do twirls in the air like Peggy Fleming. Often she would get upset at me for dropping crumbs or spilling milk on her spotless floors.

Then angrily she would slap me across the face and call me a "cocksucker." She loved using the language of the streets. Once I was lying in her bed because I was sick and I happened to open my eyes as she was naked, in the process of getting dressed, and she yelled, "You fucking peeping Tom!" I don't know: I think deep down she really enjoyed my looking at her huge breasts and her black box underneath; however, I believe for some reason she carried a huge anger in her heart.

So now her beauty is gone. Her hair is unkempt and looks like a patched grey wig on a soiled mannequin. Her face is so wrinkled that it looks like hundreds of tiny waves in the sand formed by a gusting and swirling beach wind. She walks with a walker because of two hip replacements. The sexy swinging hips of yesterday were gone and replaced by a slow, unsteady shuffle.

Seven days a week I serve her breakfast in bed. Her OCD is more severe than ever. Everything has to be perfect, or she will become wildly agitated. The breakfast routine consists of a handful of multi-grain cereal with exactly six ounces of 2% milk and warmed for exactly thirty-five seconds in the microwave, one half cup of prune juice warmed for twenty seconds in the microwave, two slices of lightly buttered wheat toast, and so on and so on. For years, this has been the routine. When I am not available, Kathy, my wife, or, if unavailable, one of the caregivers substitute for me. The same order and routine went for meals: Monday – chicken with rice; Tuesday – ham soup; Wednesday – pork chops with broccoli soup; Thursday – macaroni with meatballs and sausage; Friday – fish sandwich from McDonald's with sweet potato fries that we cooked. On and on it goes, along with cleaning her bedroom twice a day because of her fear of bugs and contamination. Our job is to prevent some disaster from happening. Often I dream of her being terminally ill and the doctors would ask me if I want resuscitation, a ventilator, or a feeding tube. I would refuse. If she developed Alzheimer's disease, I would also refuse any type of nutrition or hydration.

Overall, her mind is still razor sharp. However, I read in a medical journal that her OCD is also a form of dementia. Sometimes I wish for Alzheimer's so her rituals would be forgotten. Her doctor, a forty-year-old good looking Italian with a muscle-toned body, says she had a heart of a forty-year-old and that she is so cute. Little does he know how this cute bitch is splitting my wife and me apart.

My wife, Kathy, before we began to take care of my mother, was athletic, perky, and full of life. However, after ten years of taking orders from my mother like a personal secretary and chef, Kathy is spent and running on empty. Her deep blue eyes have lost their sparkle and her body is fading quickly as her clothes just hang on her.

My father, who died five years ago of a major stroke, told me in his last years that her demands were killing him. Every night he would have to get up as she yelled, "Mike, Mike, help!" It was always the same. He said he had to straighten up the covers so that they didn't twist around her delicate feet. On several occasions he said to me he would've left her if it wasn't for me. He also said old man Edwards who owned the department store was bedding her. That's why he said they went together to New York and bought clothes. He didn't care anymore because he also had a "special friend."

My mother made it clear to us that she would not go into a nursing home or an assisted living facility. She said my father told her if she did we would steal all of her money. I just don't understand how my father, a Syracuse University graduate in finance, would think that. Through his investments, he left her well off. I think he thought she was going to die first, but as she said to me, "I fooled that son of a bitch." Of course knowing my mother's proclivity to lie, she could've made that up—the stuff about stealing money. On the other hand, my dad also lied to me about his money. I knew he had IBM stock, but he said he had very few. After he died, we found a statement in his safety deposit box listing one million dollars worth. But the real shock came to me when I was cleaning out the attic. My mother told me she wanted all of his clothes, or anything he had, to be gone. She wanted no trace of him. I figured they both knew of their lovers. Anyway, as I was cleaning out the attic, I found an old suitcase that seemed heavy, and when I opened it, I found over a million dollars in cash. It now is buried underneath a 100-year oak tree in the backyard. I often wonder how he got that money but then I think I don't care. I will surprise Kathy with it after my mother dies.

When I look in the mirror now, like Kathy, my clothes hang on me. I look like a ghost of what I looked like a few years ago. My mother is like a chronic disease eating away at us bit by bit. Finally I convinced her that Kathy looked awful and needed a break. My mother said that was bullshit because Kathy was always going to lunches with her friends, shopping, and enjoying herself. Anyway, she agreed because she needed a break from us, she said. Whatever. We got a 30-day respite from her. She went to Holy Family Assisted Living Facility and we went to an oceanfront home in Hilton Head. It took about a week to really unwind but we became close again as we watched the sunsets and walked the beach early in the mornings. In the second week Kathy began to look like her old self. Her beauty and body were coming back to shape. I even noticed my depleted body coming back. As I look back on it now it would be the last time we were truly happy. There was no way out after my mother came back from Holy Family. The routine began again and it was even more severe than before. Now she announces everything she is going to do: I gotta pee; I'm exercising; I have to move my bowels; I can't go—I'm constipated; I am going to bed; Kathy, I will call you to give me a bath....

Like Kathy, I have no fight left in me and so we both become totally submissive to her every order.

The grand jury begins with my background. The assistant prosecuting attorney looks like a fat fish with slits as eyes and a wide mouth. His name is Joe Shaffer.

Shaffer: State your name.

Witness: Andrew Prentiss.

Shaffer: What do you do for a living?

Witness: I used to teach at Hobart and William Smith Colleges.

Shaffer: What do you do now?

Witness: Until my mother died, we took care of her.

I choke with emotion and feel my eyes get watery.

Shaffer: Can you tell me what happened on the morning of December 21st?

Witness: My wife and I were going to take her to her favorite restaurant, IHOP. However, it was a very long and involved process to take her anywhere.

Shaffer: What do you mean?

Witness: Well, first we had to get her dressed with layers of clothing like sweaters, coat, scarf, hat, gloves, then I had to use a heavier wheelchair to transport her to the car; the lighter wheelchair I put in the car's trunk so when we got to IHOP I could use that one.

Shaffer: Now, Mr. Prentiss, tell me where your wife was as you were getting her into the wheelchair?

Witness: She was helping me lift her from her lazyboy chair to the wheelchair.

Shaffer: Once you got her into the wheelchair, what did you do then?

Witness: I wheeled her from the living room toward the front porch. My wife held the living room door open while I tilted the wheelchair back so I could make it over the threshold to the porch.

Shaffer: Then what?

Witness: With the chair still tilted back and my wife helping as much as she could, I wheeled her over the threshold on to the porch.

Shaffer: Then what?

Witness: With the chair still tilted back, I headed toward the steps leading down to the sidewalk. My wife was helping at the side.

Shaffer: How many steps down from the porch?

Witness: Two.

Shaffer: Is it true your wife has a bad back?

Witness: Yes.

Shaffer: Okay, go on.

Witness: I tripped ever so slightly on a small opening between the porch floor boards and like that my mother fell out of the wheelchair.

I begin to choke with emotion again. The memory is so vivid of her screaming as she fell, "Oh God, help me!"

Shaffer: You want a little break here?

Witness: No, I want this over.

Shaffer: Where did her head hit?

Witness: On a large, round rock on the edge of the sidewalk. That rock is like all of the rocks that surround both sides of the sidewalk. Anyway, quickly I went to her and placed her head in my lap and told my wife to call 911. There was little blood but a lot of white stuff was coming out. The doctors told me later it was muscles from the brain.

I was shaking now, crying almost uncontrollably.

Shaffer: Andy, let's take a little break now.

Witness: No, I want to finish because if I didn't trip she would be here. It's my fault she died.

Shaffer: Okay, how long did it take for the ambulance to get there?

Witness: I don't know. They were quick, 5 or 10 minutes. I went with her in the ambulance to the hospital. She died in my arms on the way.

Shaffer: Mr. Prentiss, do you feel responsible?

Witness: As I said, yes, I do. I have to live with this for the rest of my life.

Joe Shaffer is quiet for about five minutes as he looks through his notes. I think how hot it is in the courtroom. The courthouse itself is a plain, bricked square building and it seems over a hundred years old. It is shabby but functional. I figure the air conditioning is old, especially in the courtroom.

Shaffer: Is it true that you will inherit close to two million dollars?

Witness: I guess. My lawyers are working on that.

Shaffer: Mr. Prentiss, did you purposefully let your mother fall? In short, did you plan this whole thing and want to kill her?

Witness: Oh God, no! I loved my mother, even though she drove me crazy at times. I loved her!

I am sobbing again as Shaffer studies his notes and then brings his head up and sternly asks:

Shaffer: Don't you think it's questionable, Mr. Prentiss, that for at least ten years you've been going down those stairs with her in the wheelchair but this time you tripped?

Witness: Yes, but I would never kill my mother.

Shaffer: Mr. Prentiss, is there any other money you are not telling us about?

Witness: No.

Shaffer: Your father was a shrewd banker, right?

Witness: Yes, but he was honest, truly honest.

Shaffer: Any money hidden?

Witness: No, absolutely not. Also, I did not kill my mother. I tripped and feel terribly responsible. But, I didn't do it on purpose. I mean it. I wouldn't do that!

Shaffer: We'll see. Mr. Prentiss, the grand jury will decide if there's enough to indict. You understand?

Witness: Yes.

On the drive home, Kathy asks, "Do you think there will be a trial?"

"No, I think that was it."

"I hope so. I can't take much more."

I lovingly touch her cheek. "Everything will be okay, hon."

When we arrive home, Kathy goes downstairs to our bedroom. I go to the refrigerator and get a bottle of wine. I pour a glass and sip at it as I look out as darkness falls over the woods in our backyard. I just want peace now. Quiet is what we both need. Our house phone rings. I pick it up and pace as I talk.

"Mr. Prentiss." Shit, I think, Shaffer.

"Yes."

"This is Joe Shaffer. I wanted you to know that the grand jury decided to indict you for the murder of your mother. The trial will begin in two months."

"I can't believe it," I angrily say. "It was an accident."

"Anyway, have your lawyer call me."

I hang up and finish the glass of wine and then go downstairs. I think about how nice it was after the funeral: we slept in, went out to eat when we wanted to. We even went to Hilton Head for two weeks and enjoyed ourselves but not like before. Something was missing.

As I walk into the bedroom, I see Kathy lay curled up on our bed with a bright orange afghan over her. My mother gave it to us years ago for one of our anniversaries.

"Who was that on the phone, Andy?"

"The prosecuting attorney."

"What did he want?"

I lie down next to her and lay my arm over her as she now faces me.

"They indicted me."

"Andy, did you really trip?"

"Yes," I lie. "Really, Kath, do you think I would do that to my mother?"

"I know. I am just so tired from her, the funeral, and now we have to go through a trial."

"Don't worry, we will be okay," I lie again.

How could they prove anything? I think to myself. It was perfect. You see, nursing homes or assisted living facilities are the new killing fields in America. Millions of murders happen yearly in these places with very few people being caught. Old people fall often so who knows if they were pushed or really have fallen? My mother could've also become disabled, and we would have had no choice but to place her in a nursing home. I was fatigued from the craziness, the bitchiness, the Ritual, the Order, the OCD…day after day.

"Kath, don't worry," I say as I bring her close to me.

We have gentle and slow sex. Afterwards, I think we are finally free and we will never have to worry about money. I have the inheritance and the oak-tree money. First, I think I will buy a home in Hilton Head and we will leave our troubles behind us. Then I will buy a new car, a boat…perhaps go to Italy and live there each year for several months. I want to live on the magnificent Lake Como.

I awake in the middle of the night and go upstairs to my mother's bedroom. I can smell her flowered powder she used nightly. Then I go to the living room and smell her there because of the fourteen hours a day she sat in the dark blue lazyboy. Everything about the room, her kleenex, her pillows on the chair, everything says to me she still is here. However, I know in reality she is gone and we have to sell the house. In a way, she filled my days with hell, but something tells me I am going to miss her, especially during the coming fall. She loved the cool evenings and the smell of crushed leaves.

In Vitro

Last night he dreamed about his son being made with a beautiful woman. In the dream, however, he could not find the hospital his son was in. He kept going up and down the elevator sweating with nerves. He never found his son as it ended with him being stuck between floors. He wanted a son so badly, even though considering his circumstances, it was now almost impossible. And yet he has reached a point he wanted a child, especially a son, more than anything else. He knew if he had a son his life would be more than it is now. To him, it seemed so simple: Find a woman, and then Bang, one night he would get her pregnant, and then Bang, nine months later like a tulip bursting forth out of a bulb. However, for the last ten years, he had been the associate pastor of St. Francis in Cortland, New York. He loved the beautiful sloping mountains that surrounded Cortland, which lost most of its manufacturing to the cheap labor of the South. Basically, it had become the bedroom community of Syracuse, twenty miles north on Route 81. Most of the jobs that now existed in Cortland were low-paying at Wal-mart and fast food restaurants.

The parishioners of St. Francis loved Father Jim Crowley. He visited the sick; counseled couples who were getting ready to have babies or marry; baptized the young and old; prepared children to receive communion; and buried the dead. Not only did he want a son, he wanted to leave the priesthood soon. His bishop was a pure asshole who made unreasonable demands like identifying gays and lesbians in the parish. Also he was to seek counseling from the bishop's staff if he was enjoying sexual arousal. Artificial birth control was never to be suggested, even though some Catholic couples had seven or eight kids. He also hated the outdated rectory life. Presently, the pastor, Father Bather, was eighty-five and still lived in the rectory, even though he was diagnosed with Alzheimer's disease five years ago. Full disclosure was not the way of the church; it was cover-ups and dishonesty. Over the years, he had lived with at least three pedophile priests who eventually left but remained in the diocese somewhere in the rural parts of the state. He had heard there was a secret society called "The True Way," made up of very conservative bishops, priests, and rich businessmen, all male. This secret-society culture protected the blind belief in church authority.

Father Crowley's schedule didn't change much from day to day. He would get up at 5 a.m. and then come down from his room to the rectory kitchen. From the outside, the rectory was stone and boxy, resembling a mid-twentieth century high school with three floors. It had so many rooms that he had not seen them all. Many priests, nuns, and special church people would stay. His room had a double bed and a nightstand with a milk-glass lamp on it. In one of the far walls stood a small mahogany dresser. The bathroom was also very plain with only a sink and shower. He knew when he came into the kitchen that Mary would be waiting. She was in her sixties with a plump figure and pleasant smile. She cooked for him and Father Bather, and any other guests. Sometimes she did some typing for him. As he sat at a huge dining room table, he began to eat his cereal, toast, and drink his coffee. Today, she talked about going out with a married man even though she promised her dying husband a few years ago she would not do that. But she liked her gin and tonics and she went out and got drunk with a redneck kinda guy and he fucked her. She now knelt beside where Crowley sat and wanted to go to confession and be forgiven. She said the redneck was gentle with her but she quickly left in the morning feeling terribly guilty that she let down her dead husband, Ernie. Crowley absolved her and finished eating his breakfast. Her sister Margaret would come in later to help her clean the huge rectory. Sometimes Father Bather would come down or Mary would bring a tray up to him. It was difficult for him to go downstairs because he had bad hips.

Once he was done with breakfast he would go over to the church, which was next door, and perform the six o'clock mass. Usually after mass he would see Eva who was in her fifties with brownish, teased hair cupping her attractive face. Her body was slender, with full breasts. Eva helped with the religious education curriculum and training the Sunday school teachers to implement the program. In the afternoon she would say her rosary with her friends and afterwards she visited Mrs. Hagan at the nursing home because her family never came to visit. After mass, Eva came back to the small room where he got out of the priestly vestments. Today, she seemed depressed.

"What's wrong?" he asked.

"Nothing," she said.

"Are you sure?"

"I don't know," she said. "I'm starting to get bored with teaching. I'm looking for other challenges. I know I have so much talent that I could be using."

"What would you like to try?"

"I don't know, and even though the church doesn't pay me very much, it helps in paying off one of my children's student loans."

"I wish I could help, but as you know priests don't get very much. Basically, I get $500 a month. But I know other priests get so much more because they take from the Sunday and Christmas collections. Everything about the money is so covered up in the church."

Suddenly he thought about wanting a son and maybe she could help.

"Look, why don't you come over to the rectory after supper and we'll have a glass of wine and talk more?"

"I would like that. I was going to ask you if we could talk."

He decided as he got into the car to go visit the sick at St. Joseph's hospital, then he would see what Eva felt about his plans to father a baby boy. He would teach him to play baseball and football. He would travel to hockey games in Syracuse or maybe go to two or three games to see the Yankees or Knicks. His father was always too busy with his grocery store to ever do those things. Hopefully, his son would look like him with black wavy hair, a strong and wide chin, and sparkling black eyes. He loved to babysit babies because their smell was so pure and innocent. It was intoxicating to him. It made him sick to think of those priests who took advantage of young children. For the most part he thought the majority of priests were good people, but because of the church's hierarchy, they're left alone nightly without any opportunity for companionship. They look, he thought, to the bottle for help or search out young innocent children for human touch. Some can live being celibate while others cannot. When will the church accept that close to 70% of priests today are gay and performing their duties quite well? Last week, a former nun whom he was good friends with received a letter from Bishop Asshole saying she was going to be excommunicated if she continued to support an organization called "Call for Action." It supported what he and other priests believed in, such as gay and lesbian life, and freedom for priests and nuns to marry. Many in the group also believed in the ordination of women as priests. The letter she received said that their views are unacceptable and she must ask for mercy from the Asshole and make a public renunciation. That's why he couldn't wait to leave. But he wanted to have his son. The sex with Eva he thought would be good also. Some affairs he had these last few years were for touch and release of sexual energy.

That night Eva came over dressed in tight black slacks with a multicolored revealing blouse. Over this she wore a long, knitted black sweater with white pearls hanging down to her waist. She sat down on the overstuffed greyish sofa in the huge living room with dark molding and oak floors. He poured a glass of wine for him and her as he sat down next to her.

"Thanks, Father, for seeing me."

"Well I also wanted to see you, remember?"

"I just can't rest thinking every night if I'm going to have enough money to pay my bills. I get so depressed thinking about it, and I'm bored, like I said." She sipped at her wine and tears welled up a little.

"How much do you need?"

"To clear everything, about $50,000."

"That's a lot, but maybe I could help."

"You know," she said, "I just want the freedom to maybe start my own bookstore with books explaining all different religions."

Crowley thought of the inheritance his mother and father left him. It was close to $500,000.

"Here's the deal. I know it sounds crazy, but I want a baby boy. I'm leaving the church soon."

"I always thought you would leave, but why a baby?"

"I deserve to be a father and carry on my name. Someone would remember me through my son. You know what I mean?"

"Yes, but who would you want to make the baby with?"

"I thought about you."

"I am honored, but I had a hysterectomy a year ago and everything has been cleaned out."

"Oh, I didn't know."

She moved closer to him.

He moved toward her now and kissed her softly on the lips and soon they had their clothes off and were making love.

Afterwards, she said, "So you want a baby?"

"Yes," he said as both of them dressed.

"You know, Father, I always cared for you, especially after I heard your sermon on love that really is God in us."

"Right now until I leave the church our relationship has to be discreet."

"I know. Look, my daughter Beth is nineteen and a sophomore at Cortland State. Let's see if she can help. I know she thinks the world of you. She told me how she wishes she had you as a real father, not the one who left when she was three—remember, I've had a lot of men before I started to come to church seriously."

"That's fine. I don't care."

"Maybe she would be willing to do something like in vitro as long as it doesn't disturb her education except for a week or two. She really wants to work as an art teacher with small kids."

"Sounds good to me," he said. "Let's do it."

He thought about the Catholic church being against in vitro fertilization. He had had several couples who wanted to use the process. In vitro fertilization is the process of fertilization through manually combining an egg and sperm in a laboratory dish, then transferring the embryo to a woman's uterus, like Beth's.

The next day as he came down to breakfast Mary complained about Father Bather, "Earlier, he came down with just his t-shirt and started grabbing my breasts until I pushed him away and I brought him back up to his room. It's so sad."

"I'm so sorry. Again, I will talk to the bishop and see if he can go to Our Lady of Perpetual Help, which is for older priests and nuns who have Alzheimer's."

"Father, do you think I committed a sin because for a second I enjoyed his touching my breast?"

"God is very forgiving. Forget about it. You were just being kind."

"Thank you," she said with watery eyes.

Later, as he was taking off his vestments, Eva came in.
"Hi."

"Hi. I talked to Beth and told her how much I liked you, Father. She'll do it."

"Great."

"She asked what if we find out it's going to be a girl?"

"We try again."

"That means an abortion for Beth. I don't know if she would do that."

"Hey, let's give it a shot first. Then we'll go from there."

"Once we know it's going to be a son I'm ready to leave. I have so much disillusionment with the church's hierarchy and its doctrine on sex and the importance of the hocus-pocus at mass. Most of all, having to live with priests who are jerks. Look at poor Father Bather. He needs help. I also had a couple of pedophiles who lived with me. I reported them and they still remained until one of the church people told the bishop she was going to the press. You see, I believe what St. Paul said, 'It's no longer I who live, but Christ who lives in me.'"

Eva grabbed him and kissed him hard on the lips. "You are a brave man, Father Crowley."

He broke the embrace and said, "Call me Jim, Eva. We will be opening a portal to a new world."

After she left, he thought about how many baptisms he had performed, marriages and funerals, confessions he had heard, too many to remember. He thought, too, he couldn't feel he was acting in the power of Christ and the Holy Spirit. It also pissed him off he only got five hundred dollars a month to live on while pastors got all the money. They lived like kings. Also, he didn't believe anymore in the Pope's infallibility. It's all crap, he thought. Like the Bible; he also knew it was full of metaphors and great stories but not absolute truths.

He met Beth the next night when she came over to the rectory with her mother. She looked like Eva but with smaller features like thin lips and a smaller, but cute, nose that went along with a slim body. Her hair was long, straight, and sandy brown.

After some small talk, he asked quickly, "Beth, are you ready for this?"

"I think so," she said, "as long as I finish school on time. I think it would be kinda neat to carry a baby."

"Yeah, neat," he laughed.

Soon afterwards, once the IVF took, they found after two months it was going to be a boy. He was ecstatic and deeply in love with Eva. However, in the fifth month of pregnancy, the doctors discovered a problem with the baby's heart and said it may not make it to birth. Soon, he asked Beth to have an abortion but she said no. She wanted to go full term. In her heart, she felt the baby would come out okay. Of course, he felt just the opposite.

One night he went over to her student apartment to try to convince her again to get an abortion. Instead they ended up making love. He was now in love with both Eva and Beth. The baby boy was born four months later at 9 pounds 10 ounces. The day of the birth, he explained to Eva what happened between himself and Beth. She was fine as long as he would live with both of them and love both of them naturally and equally. She didn't mind. Exchanging partners, she felt, was the pluralistic nature for all of humanity. "Deep down," she said, "I always felt that monogamy was unnatural and a charade." He also agreed with her because for several years after listening and counseling married couples, he knew being monogamous was a myth as church history showed in current documents.

Their son, Billy, didn't really need a transplant. Their love grew deeper and strong among each other. Soon he had a baby girl, Shasta, with Beth. She had finished school, so she enjoyed carrying Shasta even more. After he left the Catholic church, he began what he called the *Church of Tomorrow*. He preached about the new marriages of two or three partners for gays, lesbians, and for everyone. He preached that it was a new day as we rewrite Christianity for a new world. The old Christianity was dead. The *Church of Tomorrow* began with ten people and in two months he had over five hundred coming to his services. Father Crowley's vision included a compassionate understanding for all people, for all faiths. True religion, he preached, was no religion. We are talking about the reconstruction of Christianity.

———————◦•◦———————

Miss Sullivan

She lived across the street from me. I hardly ever saw her except when she asked me to cut her lawn or rake leaves. Then, in the early fifties, I was sixteen, thin, short, with wavy-cut black hair and an angular face. Her name was Miss Sullivan. She was in her late thirties, frail, with deadly pale skin and wore her long greyish hair always in a ponytail. She wore dark colored dresses or sometimes black slacks with a button up white blouse. We were studying Emily Dickinson in school and her photograph reminded me of Miss Sullivan, especially the shyness in her looks. The neighbors said she wrote poetry like Emily. Also, I knew she was the major caregiver of her father who was in failing health. Some said he was dying of cancer. Later I learned she had gone away to be a nun at age twelve but had to come home at age sixteen because her mother was also dying of cancer. She died a few years later.

From my bedroom window I would watch her carefully bring her father onto the tiny porch of their small two-story home with light green siding. They had recently moved in. So little was known about them except my father said he heard that they came from New York City, and she hardly went out. I wondered why they moved from an exciting city like New York to a boring little place like Owasco, New York. All we were known for was being the home to Owasco Lake, one of the Finger Lakes, and one of the largest prisons in New York, which held the bank robber Willie Sutton.

We lived in an apartment over a grocery store that my mom and dad ran twelve hours a day, seven days a week. I was an only child and spent most of my time in my bedroom reading and daydreaming about girls, baseball, and now Miss Sullivan. At night she worked for hours in the flower garden, which ran in front of her house. I really don't know the names of flowers, but their colors were yellow, pink, red, white, and some were even multicolored. I loved watching her move swiftly but skillfully, up and down, bending at the knees. She sometimes caught me looking at her from my bedroom window. Now and then she would wave and, embarrassingly, I would wave back.

Behind her house stood a run-down barn with aged grey planks. Years ago, horses, pigs, and cows were kept there. On the side of the house, Miss Sullivan worked in a vegetable garden along with a few fruit trees.

I stayed in because my parents felt they didn't want me to be polluted by the other immigrant children in the area, Polish, Irish, Germans, and on the fringe of the neighborhood, Blacks. I didn't mind because I enjoyed reading and listening to the Yankees play on the radio and to the conversations of the Cummings, who lived next door, talking nightly on their front porch. Their talking and laughing was loud and boisterous. I was an observer, not a doer. So I loved it. I also loved watching the shadows of Miss Sullivan as she moved about in front of her second floor bedroom window covered with sheer curtains. Deep down, I felt she enjoyed being looked at. I noticed that sometimes, when she worked in the vegetable garden, she wore a huge floppy straw hat with a neatly pressed black dress that seemed to lightly outline her thin figure with its pint-sized breasts. As I said, in school I was reading Emily Dickinson, who wrote about the possible love affairs she had with a minister and a judge. I wondered if Miss Sullivan had lovers.

Today, as I was watching Miss Sullivan bring her father onto the porch, she waved up to me to come over. I jumped off my bed and quickly went over. She would be my Emily, and I would be her judge or minister, I thought. She had on a dark maroon skirt with a button up, white blouse with a small white marble pin at the top of her thin neck. In her soft and pleasing voice, she asked if I would cut the grass because it was getting too long. I was to use their push mower that was in the barn. The barn was also where Miss Sullivan kept her older green Buick La Sabre. I hardly ever saw her drive except on weekends to pick up groceries.

Today was hot and she said if I got too hot to come in and she would get me a cool glass of water. I decided at some point I would do that because I wanted to see the inside of her house. As I left to pick up the lawn mower, her father nodded and just stared ahead. He looked to be in a dazed state, but you could tell he was a man with a body in fairly good shape. He held himself with dignity and a posture that reminded me of someone who had stature and once probably held high positions in society before death came along and began to ravage him. Later on, as I became overheated by the mowing and thought of her invitation for a cool glass of water, I decided to knock on the front door. She peeked out at me as she pushed back the sheer curtains on the upper part of the door. She smiled as she opened the door, and I went inside. She motioned for me to follow her. I smelled something great cooking, like a spicy sauce with oregano and other herbs like that.

"I'm making salmon for my dad in a special hollandaise sauce," she said.

"Smells good," I said.

"Thanks. I love to cook but hate to clean." *God*, I thought, *I'm so much taller than her.*

She took a large glass out of the cupboard, placed it under the faucet, and, once filled, she handed it to me. I followed her to what looked like a den or study. I noticed as we passed her living room that it was wallpapered in a flowered print with a dark red background. The furniture looked comfortable and overused. Her den/study overlooked the barn and backyard. The walls were lined with bookcases and full of books that I thought she probably read. She told me to sit down in an over-stuffed light blue chair with a matching ottoman. She sat at her curved–spoke, wood chair in front of a half-opened large desk with piles of paper neatly stacked on top.

"Do you like to read, Joey?" she asked.

"Yes," I answered.

"Well, so do I, and I have bookshelves of classics, religion, and poetry. Anytime you would like to borrow one, please feel free to take one."

"Okay."

She had deep brown eyes that penetrated as she spoke to me. I had very few people really look at me like that.

"Do you believe in God?"

"Yes. I think sometimes he forgets about us."

"How old are you?"

"Sixteen."

"You see, I believe God is the energy of the universe, and we all are connected and fully God."

"I need to think about that." I thought, *I don't understand.* I finished my water, got up, and began to leave. She also got up, came over, and gave me a hug that made my body shiver, and that made me feel something good was happening.

"Would you like me to teach you about a new way of looking at God?"

"Sure."

"Well, come on over about the same time tomorrow."

"Okay." I thought how this summer was going to help me get away from the boringness, because I was excited and thrilled by her. She was bright.

The next day she said, "Don't be concerned where you find truth, for all of it comes from the same source. You can be in charge of your own destiny. Every version of God is part mask, part reality. The infinite can only reveal a portion of itself at one time."

I said, "So, we are always trying to discover God. Right?"

"Right. You are now on the road to what some call enlightenment."

"Jesus, I like this."

"You see, you got to lose your ego," she said, "and be like a camera with the shutter always open and stop thinking. Just let things be."

I thought she was so bright and I couldn't wait to learn more tomorrow.

But then, like that, I didn't see her the rest of the summer. I thought maybe she was mad or maybe she had problems with depression. I just didn't know but I wanted more of her wisdom.

Then, in late October, after the first snow, she came to her bedroom window and waved for me to come over.

We met on the porch. She was dressed as if it was summer. She hugged herself tightly and shivered. She had on a yellow print sleeveless dress. Also she looked like she had lost weight for the dress hung on her. She told me after I finished shoveling to come in and she would have some hot chocolate for me. Afterwards, as I went into her study, I could see on her desk her beautiful handwriting on a yellow legal pad and also newly sharpened pencils. She was drinking hot tea as I drank the hot chocolate. She seemed distant and cold as she looked over to me.

"I have made some discoveries since we last met."

"Like what?"

"From the time of Christ to the present day, culture and consciousness developed through many stages of development. In each stage, there is a new way of relating with God, a new way of living. You know what I mean?"

"I think." I thought now that she was the brightest woman in the world and I was in love with someone who was visiting from heaven.

"Joey, have you ever read Shakespeare?"

"Yes, sometimes the language is too hard."

"Well, let me read you one of his sonnets: 'See how she leans her cheeck upon her hand./ O that I were a glove upon that hand that I might/ Touch that cheek./ My bounty is as boundless as the sea./ My love as deep;/The more I give to thee/ The more I have, for both are infinite.' He is willing to give his all-consuming life for her soul and love. You understand?"

"I don't know."

"Have you ever, even at your age, experienced love like that?"

"I don't think so." I thought: *maybe now with you. You are the purest spiritual person I know.*

"Joey, I have, you know, loved a friend like that, but she killed herself."

"Oh, my God. Why did she do that?" *So,* I thought, *like Emily, she had a lover.*

"She couldn't give me the Shakespeare kind of love."

I got up, went over to her chair, hugged her, and began to rub her back for a long time. She was so spiritual, and I would not go any further, even though deep down the animal desires were stirring.

She gently pulled away, got up, and said, "You see, Joey, through relationships, we can cultivate consciousness and wisdom. So we need each other if we want to grow."

As I left I thought she was a saint and so wise too. I needed to express myself. My head was bursting with her thoughts.

One of the last times I saw her she reminded me, "Joey, I am interested in an integral stage, where with each other you and I have God. God energy keeps everything in existence."

"So, you and I are God?" I asked.

"Yes, in a way." Her blouse was unbuttoned, revealing her pure white skin. I put my hand on her skin underneath the top of her blouse and began to move toward her breasts that were hardening. She groaned, but I felt it was wrong and suddenly took away my hand. Something was "awakening" in me. Something higher; it was my soul connecting with hers.

At the door, she said: "We have in a way experienced the big bang, stirring in our love, Joey. That is the mystery in us." She then kissed me with closed lips on mine as she swung with me hard back and forth, back and forth. I didn't want it to end. When I left I was not terribly steady on my feet and when I got home I had to hold on to the furniture. I was excited, I mean out of this world excited. I could barely breathe as I ran to my room and quickly closed the door. Suddenly, I thought about my hand touching her lily white skin, peeking at her rounded breasts in silken cups. Trembling, my blood was hotly running through my veins. I just don't know what it was but I thought I was at the highest level of humanhood. I couldn't wait to see her again. She kept the shades down on her bedroom window. Her father died a month later, and I saw her dressed all in black getting into a huge Cadillac. She nodded to me from the window as I slightly waved to her. The house was sold and she moved. The movers came and took the furniture, but she wasn't around. I never saw her again.

Several years later, when I was in graduate school at Columbia, my parents called and said they had a letter at home for me. Also, the return address was from Clara Sullivan, Florence, Italy. I asked them to send it to me immediately.

Once I got the letter, I quickly opened it and read:

"Dear Joey:

"I hope you are doing well. I have lived in Florence, Italy, for several years. I teach English in a school for American children. I love the art, the music, and the opera of Florence. Everything brings me to a heightened level of meaning. There are several people here searching like me for an esoteric level of knowledge. I often think of you and think you have probably grown up to be a handsome young man. Something from Shakespeare fits what we had: 'my bounty is as boundless as the sea,/ My love as deep; the more I give to thee/ The more I have,/ For both are infinite.' Please don't write back or try to contact me because I'm moving to another part of the city.

"I just wanted to thank you for that special moment in my life…We had esoteric sips of sacramental wine, as Emily Dickinson once said.

"Love, Clara Sullivan."

That night I packed my clothes, got out my passport, and booked a flight to Florence. I don't care what she said. I will look all over Florence for her. Since our time, I have had several love affairs. All meant nothing to me. "Clara," I love saying her first name. She is my dark lady. Her memory in me is more alive than ever before. Whatever it takes, we will be together again. We will touch each other's cheeks and be one with God's energy. My love is as a high fever, burning with desire and connection. Thinking of her forces me to tremble, as I light up as a neon. I know what it means now to set my soul free.

Like her, now I have become a poet:

> We were two seeds
> Blown together into flight
> By the breezes of humanity.
> Gently coming to rest
> Upon each other in a
> Field of celestial bliss,
> Jolted into the heavens
> By the raging wind
> And throwing us askew,
> Mindfully aware that
> My flight was now alone
> And that was the
> Reality of our lives.

———⊳•⊲———

Going Home

She had golden hair and deep blue eyes. Stunning. I turned and saw her as she brushed my back with her breasts, sending a sexual shiver throughout my body. We talked about nothing as is normally done at Christmas parties. On and on it went. Both of us, I know, were thinking *how do we get beyond this shit?*

Her name was Jane Summers. I met her briefly one other time at the docking area where I docked my boat. Someone introduced us as I was leaving. I remembered she told me she owned a wine and cheese shop at a local mall. I also remembered thinking she seemed lonely and troubled.

My wife came up to us at the party and said she had a Christmas gift for Jane and that someday I would deliver it. My wife, Susan, was a cute brunette with a fading cheerleader figure. She believed in giving gifts to neighbors at Christmas time.

That was the kind of woman she was. Pleasant. Kind. And compassionate. Just plain nice. I was a computer programmer at a large pharmaceutical company in Wheeling, West Virginia.

For some reason, I couldn't get Jane out of my mind the following week. Sex is what I thought I wanted, or was it something deeper? Like any other married man, I had my share of affairs. Casual. Wild. And over in a few months. Anyway, I loved my wife very much while craving wild, forbidden sex with others. Just before Christmas, I called Jane one evening, and I said I was coming by to drop off her gift. She said she also had a gift for us.

That evening, we awkwardly exchanged gifts, and then, out of nowhere, I kissed her hard on the lips. Soon after, our bodies were pressing into each other as our tongues twisted crazily around. Then, quickly, I began to leave.

She said, "You better call me and I mean it." We were outside now. A full moon shone behind her, and the beams caught her just right, making her look ghostly and halloweenish.

I thought at the time that I would never call her, but I did, as I thought about her penetrating blue eyes gazing at me. Something was driving me insane to be with her again. We arranged to meet at her place two days later.

She texted: "I look forward to seeing you again. I have some secrets."

Once at her place, she told me she had been married three times and raped two times by two ex-husbands. She also had a daughter who was now in an abusive relationship.

"Like mother like daughter," she nervously laughed. "Most men are looking for a quick piece of ass."

I disagreed. However, I also found out that, like me, she was an ex-Catholic and fed up with its dogmas about divorce, gays, and abortion. In short, we hated the oppressive nature of the church. Now we both sought something more spiritual that we both had found in the readings of Edgar Cayce. We liked his ideas about heaven. There is no hell, purgatory, and limbo.

Everyone starts off in heaven, Cayce said, and comes to earth for spiritual growth and enlightenment. Even Hitler-like people go to heaven and come back through reincarnation to serve others. Each time, on their journey back to earth, individuals transform to a higher level of goodness.

As we talked, we drank wine and more wine so that when we got to talking about philosophy, meditation, and unlocking our spiritual entities, we devoured each other with deep passionate kisses. Somehow, like that, we were naked and in her bed. Before I knew it, we were both having orgasms. She, I think, had three or more while I never had sex so hard, deep and almost endlessly.

Pressing hard on me, she whispered, "I'm home with my father. Can you see him? He's a chief and sitting next to me beside the tepee with our wolves as our guards."

Her hand shot up quickly as she twisted it. "See the cliffs and beautiful mountains? See the sky? Hear the sounds and smell the air. See…."

Fuck, I thought. *She's a nut case.*

I had all sorts of thoughts about bringing her to the ER with her hand frozen and twisted, arm in mid-air. I tried to gently shake her, and she began to cry uncontrollably.

"Father, I wanted to stay home with you." Finally, she slowly came back to this world as she curled up into my arms. She thanked me for bringing her to her home. She said because of my tender lovemaking she was able to stay home longer than ever before. We were in the fourth dimension.

"Did you travel with me?"

"Yes," I lied. Still, I couldn't relate to her world of chiefs and Native Americans.

The next day at work I tried to concentrate on developing a program to sort out the company's generic drugs. She texted: "I love you and thanks for opening a new portal to my home. xoxxxoo."

I texted back: "I'm afraid I need to understand what happened last night. I'm scared I'm losing myself in you. To be honest, I felt the love but I only saw the wolves baring their teeth at me."

She texted back: "Tonight you will see my home again. I need to see you or I might do something crazy to myself. Love and miss you."

Oh, my God, I couldn't let her do something crazy. I would never forgive myself.

I texted back: "I will be there, but we must really talk about the world you're going to. Right now, I'm not even sure I saw the wolves."

She texted: "I understand, hon. Everything will be clearer tonight. Can't wait. Love you forever."

When I go tonight, I thought, I will break it off and get back to the normal suburban life: going to the movies once a week, having dinner out once a week, watching football once a week, and, of course, making normal love once a week. I wanted normality, and right then she and I were living abnormal lives, even though Jane's world haunted me along with the deep love I felt for her.

That night I talked to her about my fears of her not coming back from her home. She said not to worry, that once I experience her home and fly above her world everything will be clear.

Like before, we drank and talked, drank and talked, and like that, she had me guiding her to her home again.

This time, as we made love greedily, I was swimming in a warm brown liquid as my hands, arms, body got swallowed up in her black vulva. I saw her father with his multi-colored headdress. He smiled at me as we sat outside near a bright white tepee. I had never felt such contentment and peace.

As before, it was hard for her to come back and for me it took all I could to also get back.

Later, I texted: "Last night was the scariest of all. I went through a portal where I journeyed with you through dimensions where I felt warm light and pure peace. Now all I want is for you to think about me all the time, just like me. All my love, addicted to you."

She texted: "Strange, I was wondering how you were doing after last night. The spirit for us is strong today. Tonight. I have a major surprise for you. I love you!!! P.S. I may stop by after lunch. I'm thinking about you all the time. Answer yes or no: would you take a bullet for me?"

I texted back: "Sure. All the time."

Jane stopped by my office after lunch. She ran into my assistant, Alice, coming out of the office. She is in her mid-forties and still very attractive in a classical way. A few years ago, we had a brief affair, but I called it off because of her controlling nature. By her actions, I felt she wished it was still on. When Jane came in, she angrily slammed the door closed and accused me of still having an affair. She saw cushions on the floor from my sofa and assumed something happened.

"You are like all other men!" she screamed. "I smell her perfume," she said as she approached me.

I said, "Nothing happened."

"Once I would like to trust a man!" she yelled.

"Nothing happened," I said. "Don't do this. I was working on a report with her. I love you." I grabbed her and kissed her with lust and passion and soon she stopped resisting.

"Damn you," she said afterwards. "If I find out you're cheating on me, I'll kill you," she nervously laughed.

I also laughed with a little worry.

I had some control issues when she couldn't meet one night because she was doing something with her gay friend Liz. My wife said I enjoyed being distant and also controlling. I knew I was good looking, being six two with long dark hair. I worked out often, so my chest, arms, and legs looked well chiseled. Women, I knew, were attracted to me. Some women, like Alice, saw me as being dark and haunting. Jane said she needed her gay friend and girlfriend. She didn't like being controlled. I told her I would work on it.

"I hate possessive guys."

"I understand," I said, "but because I am so busy, my time is limited also. When I'm free, I need you to be there."

"Just don't be a jerk," she said.

After such fights about my control, our lovemaking was mind-blowing and yet gentle and respectful.

She texted later that day: "I can't wait until tonight. I don't ever want to think you will be with another woman. Your wife is nice but I know you have more with me."

That night we talked about seeking newer and deeper levels of spirituality that we would travel through as we went home together. Earlier, she talked about wanting to linger or stay for good at her home. However, she worried about her daughter and would miss her.

Tonight we didn't need as much wine as our sex was more fierce than ever. She asked in the midst of our heated and passionate sex if I loved her.

I said, "Yes."

"Deeply?"

I said, "Yes" again.

"Good," she said.

Then suddenly I felt something cutting into my back. It hurt. Now I felt something stabbing at the right side of my back. Shit, it hurt like hell. There was hot liquid-like stuff dripping down my back now. It felt like I was rubbing against a barbed-wire fence. She asked again, "Do you love me?"

I said, "Yes," but wondered why now I was having a hard time breathing. I tried to push her off me and then suddenly saw a shining kitchen knife in her hands, plunging it into her heart. Soon blood began shooting out like from a powerful water hose.

As my world grew darker and darker but warm, I heard her say, "We will be home, my sweet one."

Sandy, My Love

This morning, I got the call from her best friend, Shirley.

"Did you know Sandy Charles died?"

"No. The last time I heard from her was several years ago when I was doing a play in New York."

"Well, I thought you might want to know. I know you were close to her."

"Thanks, Shirley."

I hung up the phone and began thinking about Sandy and when we met at St. Boniface Elementary School in the third grade in a small town in upstate New York. I had been asked to leave Wallace Street School in second grade.

I was the only child of an immigrant father, Patsy, who was handsome with dark black hair, a David Niven–type mustache, and short muscular body. My mother, Marion, was born to immigrant parents. She was taller than my father with a Lauren Bacall figure. My father could be mean sometimes but would cry at the drop of a hat, whereas my mother was cold and insensitive. My father owned a very successful construction company. My mother worked as a floor supervisor at a sparkplug factory. My father was also the Ward Supervisor of the neighborhood, made up of Italians, Poles, and displaced Ukrainians. When people had a problem with city services, they came to him. Because he was considered wealthy, people came to him for loans, which he secured with their homes, cars, dump trucks, watches, rings, and so on. There was a rumor that he was connected to the Mafia; however, I never saw any indication of that. At times in the late sixties any Italian who was successful was considered connected to the Mafia. Sure, my father associated with them, but only in a distant and casual way.

The principal at Wallace called my parents and asked them to come in. Her name was Mrs. McGuire. We never knew her or the teachers' first names. They were *Downton Abbey* types and we were lowly Italians, servant-like. They said I was doing good in school but I was a terrible discipline problem. I wouldn't stay in my seat. I was always bothering the other students. However, the reason my parents were asked to come in was because I had loosened some nuts on the teachers' commode so that when they flushed, instead of the water going down, it shot up like a geyser. I hid across the hall behind a half-opened door and watched with glee as the women, especially Mrs. McGuire, came out, angrily shaking their dresses.

Mrs. McGuire told my parents that I was too much to handle and suggested that the Sisters of Charity at St. Boniface could probably handle me better.

The following fall I went to St. Boniface and began third grade where I met Sandy Charles. I was given a seat in back of her and as I approached, her big brown eyes and wide grin warmed me all over. I knew something good would come of us. While I passed, I noticed her lemon-sized breasts underneath her school uniform white blouse. I was quiet all day, staring at the curve of her neck and the perfect short cut of her bluish black hair. I was in love, and it would be forever. But the problem I had was I was too shy to talk to her for any extent of time. I was much better talking to the faster girls in class. I didn't want anything to spoil my image of Sandy. She was my dream girl. Loretta and Rose were fast girls and had parties at their houses. Loretta had big breasts and she loved the boys to feel her up when we played Spin the Bottle, whereas Rose loved practicing French kissing with the boys. Both like to be humped on the back steps of the school. Sandy never came to the parties and stayed aloof from Loretta and Rose at school. She just smiled and laughed after that first day as I went back to disrupting the class.

One day, Sister Berdine caught me writing in a little black book my father had given me. I would love writing about Sandy in there. This day, I had written about her cute button-like nose and thin lips that were made for open kisses and her breasts that were made for easy cupping. Suddenly, Sister Berdine came up behind me and with her weapon of choice tapped me hard on the head with a ruler and told me to begin reading what I was writing.

Reluctantly, I stood, feeling my face burning as if I had a fever of 104 degrees. I began reading, but Sister stopped me quickly when I got to Sandy's breasts. I saw the back of Sandy's neck turning dark red.

From then on and until I graduated from the eighth grade, the nuns trained me to be a master altar boy along with bookroom boy. I went to each class and yelled "bookroom!" One time I yelled too loudly for one nun and I got slapped hard across the face. I very seldom attended class except to take tests. Most of the time I spent at the convent with Sister Aloysius, helping her cook and tend to the garden. All of this was a way to control my hyperactivity. I missed seeing Sandy and looking at her white smooth skin, not a blemish on it. I also missed looking at her lips and the delicate shape of her ears and neck. Still I loved her deeply and sometimes became thrilled when I got a Valentine card that said "love you," which I knew she sent to all the boys. However, I also knew she really meant it for me. She became the blessed Virgin to me, as I learned from Kay Castro, a plump girl, how to French kiss, massage a breast, and hump on the back steps of St. Boniface in all kinds of weather. My parents thought I was at the Community Center playing basketball, not getting thrilled by feeling the silk of Kay's bra. I knew Sandy was too pure to ever be involved in animalistic sexual activity. Her smile over the years in elementary school was always warm but not inviting. She was an angel that wanted to have a hand print on my heart forever.

We lost touch after St. Boniface, as my parents sent me off to a private exclusive military school where I learned discipline and how to study. Most importantly, my English teacher, Mr. Anderson, taught me to love literature and art. He was gay and this was in the fifties but none of us students cared because he was so inspirational. He was our Robin Williams in *Dead Poets Society*. He made literature come alive for me as a human being. I was able to gain insight into my life or confirm things I already knew. I thought of Sandy often and had heard she was going out with as many boys as she could. I wondered if she was still a virgin. I wasn't. I lost it to Lisa Epstein on her sofa. Because her parents wouldn't let her date non-Jewish boys, my name for her parents was Marshall Fienstein. I did hear Sandy was serious with one guy named Jack Kelly who was tall, blond, and would pass for Troy Donahue. Then, I heard he died of cancer.

Mr. Anderson had me read *Seven Storey Mountain* by Thomas Merton in my senior year, and I decided I would go to St. Bonaventure University and become a Franciscan. If I couldn't have Sandy, the monk's life was the only alternative. Sandy was at Rosehill College when I began college.

Soon I discovered at St. Bonaventure I couldn't ever be a monk. It wasn't the celibate life, it was the disciplined life of a monk. The rituals, the prayers, the silence, the bells were all too much for me.

The beginning of my sophomore year, I called Sandy out of the blue and asked if she would be my date for our Fall Festival. Still, I couldn't talk to her without feeling awkward and shy. But I knew once we made love on this weekend she would be mine for life. Hell, I had so many girls now that I dated three on the same weekend in my freshman year. I have grown up to be quite handsome with dark curly hair, somewhat muscular and tall. I knew once she saw me and we made passionate love I would have to beat her off me.

I decided not to make my move until after the concert. Alone in the car after the concert I decided I would park in an isolated area in the Allegheny Mountains. Then I would kiss her, strip her naked, and give her sex she would never forget.

All my friends were impressed with her stunning beauty. Every single one of my friends, even though they had dates, couldn't keep their eyes off her. They looked or gazed at her as if she were some movie star. At the dance before the concert, they fought to dance with her. I didn't care because I knew what was going to happen afterward.

Once the concert, by jazz great Dave Brubeck, was finished, we left and drove to the Allegheny Mountains. We parked in a deserted picnic area. I felt now that I could finally express my love for her. I will kiss her so that my breath becomes one with her. I placed my arm around her shoulders and pulled her closer to me as my hips pressed against the steering wheel as I tried to get her closer to my chest. I kissed her with an open mouth but her mouth remained closed. Then I tried sticking my tongue through her closed lips while my hand went for her lemon-sized breasts.

Suddenly she began to giggle and then laughing hard; crying, she was laughing so hard.

"I've never had anyone try to neck so awkwardly. You're too funny, Frankie. Let's go."

Stunned, confused, I drove off. I could tell she felt nothing for me.

The Allegheny Mountains stood against the moonlit night and seemed to be swallowing me up whole. Sitting as close as possible to the car door, I heard her softly crying.

"Frankie, I'm sorry I'm so sorry. It's not you. Something is wrong with me."

"It's okay," I lied.

Several years later when I was in New York doing one of my plays, she called and said she wanted to see me and the play. She read about the play in the *New York Times*. I told her I would have a couple of comps for her at the box office. She was coming with a friend. She was teaching at a school for the gifted in Harlem.

"Frankie, my mother told me you're a famous playwright now."

"I guess."

All night I looked for her and she never showed. Then I got the call from Shirley about her death. I called Shirley back and asked her if I could visit Sandy's home. She said that it was okay and that Sandy lived in an apartment on Park Avenue. She would leave the key with the doorman. There was a folder on her desk that I might be interested in, Shirley said.

I took a taxi to her place and kept wondering how she could afford a place on Park Avenue. Even though I now lived with my wife in the Outer Banks in North Carolina, I loved New York because of the pulsating energy of the city along with the noise, smells, and the people from all over the world. We stopped in front of a classic Greco-Roman–style apartment building on Park Avenue. In the vestibule I picked up the key from the doorman and I went up to the sixteenth floor. As I opened the door, I could see she had an affluent lifestyle. The furniture was cozy but elegant. The paintings and prints were mostly by Monet and Dali. As I looked at photos of her on the desk, she still looked beautiful except for some crow's feet around her eyes along with streaks of grey in her black hair. The photos showed her with two older people, probably her parents. There were some photos of her with an older man on a sailboat. There were also photos of her with black students in her classroom. The remaining pictures were of her and another female her age holding hands and, in one, kissing passionately in front of the New York City Courthouse. Another was signed "Love Forever, Pam." There was a *Times* article about my play being done at the Fitzgerald. There was also a post-it on the article that said "call Frankie and tell him how much I think of him and wish we can be friends now. I knew he would always make it. Pam and I will get tickets."

I called Shirley and asked outright if Sandy was a lesbian. She said yes and Sandy was going to tell you but decided against it. Sandy found out that her breast cancer had spread throughout her body after she had called me for tickets. She was very rich because her parents had left her a lot of money. Most of the money she now left to Pam, her wife of two years. They also were thinking of adopting a young black boy from the school.

"Also," Shirley said, "a guy from Xerox gave her a million dollars for the program in Harlem and for her personally. He died last year of prostate cancer. He indulged her. She loved him too."

I decided to walk back from the theatre on Broadway. Where do I go from here? I thought. Because I knew that I still loved her. It was a spiritual and passionate love I now had for Sandy. Our love was also always better in my fantasy world than reality. I hurried to the theatre and thought I now wanted to think about Sandy in order to fill in the gaps when I wasn't thinking about my writing.

The afternoon sky was dark and dreary and it looked like rain. The blaring of the horns and thud of tires going over manhole covers match the excitement I felt for Sandy. Rapid-moving streams of people flanked both sides of the clogged Broadway Avenue. I opened the doors to the theatre and said hi to the box office staff. I felt an exciting shiver move through me.

Just then Sandy whispered in my ear, "Think about me all day."

"I will."

"Good," she said.

There she was now in front of me. She looked lovely as she did thirty years ago. She had on a slim pair of pressed black slacks and a white sleeveless blouse. Her lips were wider and her eyes were bright as ever. Her black hair was long and pulled back in a ponytail, with very little makeup on her face.

I smiled and she smiled back.

Skaneateles

I met her and her fifteen-year-old daughter at a small coffee shop in downtown Skaneateles, New York. I was house-sitting for my friend Janet, staying at her cottage on the west side of Skaneateles Lake. She was staying in town because her mother was dying of cancer. After my heart operation, the doctor told me I needed to rest for at least three months. I've been through a tough divorce where my ex got everything except for my books and clothes. She was a lawyer and hated me because I committed adultery with our next-door neighbor. So that's how I ended up living in a beautiful white-cedar shingled cottage on the lake. I'm into my third week of resting. Most days I sit outside on the deck and watch the lake. Before this respite, I was an English professor at Wells College, and now I'm on a six-month sick leave. Recently I was just beginning to get bored when Janet, a colleague of mine, called about meeting Phyllis Charles and her daughter. The daughter wanted to be a model. And Janet knew that every so often I modeled for an agency in Syracuse. In a way, I represented a fairly good looking fortyish male, tall, greyish hair and not a bad looking body from years of watching what I eat and jogging almost daily. In fact, the doctor said that because I was a jogger it helped the blood get around the blocked arteries. He put in four stents on the blocked arteries. Anyway, it was good to get out and meet Phyllis and her daughter Ariel. Phyllis was perhaps in her mid-fifties. She was pretty with long legs and flowing brunette hair cupping her face. Her daughter had sandy blonde hair, huge blue eyes, but a very thin body as her clothes hung on her. She seemed dazed as Phyllis did most of the talking.

"I appreciate your taking the time to see us, Professor Duran," she said.

"Please call me Perry."

"You see, my daughter loves to dress up in a new outfit every day," she smiled as she brushed her hair back from her face. Her move was sexy. "Professor, I mean Perry, I also write and only have a G.E.D."

"That's good." I think she was more interested in talking about herself than her daughter's modeling career.

"I've been writing for a long time, but I don't know how to put them together. You know what I mean?"

"Yes."

"I have a lot of thoughts about caskets and an old man with a white beard standing near my bed." There was a quaver in her voice.

Her daughter was not listening to her mother and said, "I just like dressing up."

"Sure. Look, Ariel, why don't you email some of your photos?" Looking at Phyllis now, "And also your mommy can send some of her writings to me."

"Thank you, thank you," Mommy said happily. Phyllis was not overly built but seemed to be designed for speed and endurance. As she kept flipping her hair from her face, I noticed she seemed jittery and vulnerable.

Later that night I opened my tablet and saw an email from Phyllis with two attachments. I opened the pdf with Ariel's photos. I felt that they made her look cheap and anorexic. Then I opened the pdf with Phyllis's writings. Her writings seemed raw and troubling. I needed to study them more so I took the tablet off the dining room table and went out to the deck with a glass of wine.

The lake was like a mirror tonight as it reflected the oak trees above. The sun was setting, making it seem that the lake was setting the trees ablaze. Skaneateles Lake means "beautiful squaw," in the Onondaga's Native American language. Also, I had heard that many celebrities and presidents came to the lake to be water-cured because of how clean and pure it was.

The downtown area was also charming with its small clothing boutiques and art galleries, while homes on the lake all spoke of money.

Sitting now in a white Adirondack chair, I turned on the tablet again as the pain in my chest began. First, I saw an email from the modeling agency saying that they were not taking anyone Ariel's age because they had too many in her age category. Then I clicked onto Phyllis's writings again.

She grew weary with the fear of the constant anger and arguing among her parents in which she knew that he was going to beat her after he beat her mother. Anytime they got into an argument he would stammer up the stairs and angrily scream out her name, "Amanda," and say, "You can't hide from me...."

Her story went on and on about how her father, who is a preacher, would beat her over and over because he said she had "evil eyes." The church people thought she was possessed. He must cleanse her before she could be accepted.

In bed, she slightly rolls her head to the right side of her body and catches a glimpse of a black shadowy figure hovering over her. This thing is on her and peering down and hurts her. She is in utter terror as she releases a huge scream. He quickly leaves through the window and into the fog and this is where her pain begins...She is gripped with utter fear and tried to yell out for help but she couldn't get out any more sounds....

I took a nitroglycerin along with the wine, and it helped my chest pain to subside for a while. Back to Phyllis, I wondered how many more times she was physically or even sexually abused. *What about the daughter?* I thought. I laid down the tablet and drank some more wine. I wanted to connect to them for it might help me forget my pain and how I also blew my marriage not only with the neighbor but with having too many one-night stands. I blamed her for my looking around. After the first month of marriage, she always found an excuse to not have sex: food poisoning, sinuses, too tired, migraine headaches, and on and on it went. In fact, after three months we couldn't make serious eye contact for we knew it was over. We used euphemisms like "I missed you today" and "I love you." But it was over, and yet we stayed married for three years. Thank God, we had no kids.

"I can't have kids," she said, "because I want to be the best lawyer in the state and in the country." I drank excessively to deal with the pain of living with someone I hated and what happened with that student. The end result for me was having a major heart attack as the divorce was finalized. I knew it was coming for I had lost interest in everything. I loved to read and write for they were escapes for me, but during my low periods I found myself unable to concentrate on anything. Sometimes my dark moods would overcome me and I would become suicidal. For some reason, the heart pain still existed even after the operation. Last night the pain was terribly bad. The Ativan and Ambien helped a little. Most of all, the wine with the pills brought a little relief. I turned on the tablet again, and I began to read more of Phyllis's writings.

Slowly the lids of the casket opened up, there lying in the caskets were her mom, dad, her two brothers and her two sisters....An empty casket came to Amanda, floating around her, she knew what it was wanting. She leaped upon the casket and it started taking her through the tunnel of fire...Going further in the tunnel, she saw that skeletons were forming on the walls of the tunnel. They were falling all around her, an arm, then a leg, the bones kept falling.... Then water starts to push her upward. She loses her hold of her casket and tumbles out....

In a sense, Phyllis had some structural problems with her writings but she had an abused voice that needed to be heard. Soon afterwards, I called Phyllis and told her I wanted to meet her for lunch the next day at the Sherwood Inn. She agreed to meet me. I liked the Sherwood Inn for at one time in the 1800s it was where stagecoaches stopped for passengers to eat and sleep. Full of history.

When we met, she was wearing a tweed suit with a black sweater underneath. I asked her if she worked and she said she had been a personal trainer for over twenty years. Now I understood why she had such a good looking figure. Today, I noticed she seemed again very nervous. She was talking and going in many different directions at the same time.

"Hey, Phyllis, what's wrong?" I asked.

"Nothing."

"Are you sure?"

"Well, I was worried about what you would think about my crazy writing." Tears welled up in her eyes as our glasses of Revolutionary red wine came. It was the only wine I get drunk on now.

"Don't worry. What is it?"

She spoke with more clarity. "You know I have never dealt with why I got married at 16. I hide myself in the corners of my house because of him."

"You mean your dad? Did he sexually abuse you also?"

"I don't know," she cried a little. "I just know I'm weary of hiding. Really I view others as figments of my imagination and they scare the hell out of me. I avoid conflict and friendship like the plague. You know, come to think of it, it was sort of sexual abuse," she said with more control in her voice. "But it wasn't by my father. I was in Ohio and you know how kids are. My girlfriend and I were running all over the place. Our parents didn't care. It was a rock concert. Then these guys got us drinking and they raped us over and over. People think after being raped you are just a victim. But life goes on after, you know?" Tears began to well up in her eyes reflecting the sunlight from the outside. And now from out of the darkest and deepest part of me came something I thought I had exorcised a long time ago.

"I was also raped," I said, "by a Wells College freshman girl in my first year of teaching. I let it happen because I couldn't fight back. She was a girl. I could never hurt a girl or woman.

It's not in me to do such a thing. But I never felt so scared in my life and so damn helpless."

Phyllis said nothing, just said nothing. She gave off this feeling of an intense something concealed in her with innocence and reserve.

"I will no longer," she now said, "be silent, keeping it hidden and shameful. I want to empower others to come forward. Still, I don't know. Sometimes I talk a good game, but like now I'm trembling inside and I want to die."

I wanted to hug her and tell her I knew what she's going through. My chest pain was starting up again.

"Tell me, what do you really want to do with your life? You can't hide all the time."

"I want to write and help young people with their pain. I hate hearing about them killing themselves."

Then she changed the subject every few minutes again. We went from suicide, Jesus, her days living in Amish country, Ariel, Ariel's clothes, and so on.

Finally I asked, "Amanda, in the story, it is really you, right?"

"Yes," she stammered.

"Have you had therapy?" I asked.

"Yes, but I never told the truth. Most of those guys are jerks."

"If you want to tell your story, you have to tell the truth."

"I will, if it will help kids. I found Ariel with a bottle of pills last week. Maybe it's in her DNA, Professor, no, I mean Perry," she said, "I'm looking to you. Maybe it's wrong, but I'm trying to understand life. Help me to understand."

My pain was getting really intense. I sneaked a nitroglycerin in my mouth. It helped a little.

I told her I had to get back home because I was expecting a call from my publisher. I lied so easily.

On the way out of the Inn I told Phyllis that I would help her with her writing. I went on that her writing needed work. However, something in her writing intrigued me.

"Thank you for being willing to help. You are my mentor and leader."

"I don't know. I doubt it," I said.

She touched my shoulder as she headed in the opposite direction. There was something good about her, but also something dark looming over her.

Turning her head back to me, she said, "I'll text you tonight."

"OK," I said. I couldn't wait to get home for the wine. The pain was really intense. Then I thought about both of us and our pain. Even though we were not in the service, she, like me, perhaps had Post Traumatic Stress Disorder (PTSD). Hers was from abuse, and mine was from a failed marriage and that student. These were our traumatic events.

For so long, I had "compassion fatigue" after the heart attack where I felt resentful towards my ex, even friends and sometimes students, especially that one I hated now. That night on the deck I thought I would call Phyllis tomorrow and see if she would like to have lunch at Glen Haven Resort where for centuries people came to be cured by the cool waters of Skaneateles Lake. Perhaps she could get me back in shape by running again. Also now I had someone to talk to about being overpowered and feeling guilty that I let it happen. *That sick, sad predator thrust the bottom half of her body harder and harder onto my mouth until I could hardly breathe and eventually I lost consciousness.* Phyllis surely will understand how this black, slimy thing lives forever inside of you. Even though the pain was still there in my chest, I felt good about meeting Phyllis and having a purpose in life again. I wanted to help and be with her. She could be a good friend. I was too centered on my life, but now it was time to center on another person's life. Perhaps I could even help her daughter.

God, I thought, *what a beautiful night*. There was a bright, nearly full moon, a gentle breeze, the twinkling in the deep black sky and the smell of nearby lake wineries...it couldn't be better. Total relaxation and peace and almost no pain. I had it all this night. Even my sleep came without pills and wine. I thought I answered the phone, but I couldn't remember. I thought it was Phyllis and she wanted me to meet her at Glen Haven. How could that be? I never talked to her about that. I just didn't know because all I remembered was sleeping deeply and peacefully.

The next morning I slipped on my sweats along with my Wells College sweatshirt. I prepared the Keurig for my cup of coffee, went out and looked at the lake. My cell then rang.

"Hi," I answered.

"Perry, this is Janet. Have you heard?"

"What?"

"Phyllis shot her husband and children and then herself."

Shaking uncontrollably now, I dropped the phone, my mind turned off, and I saw only stark whiteness. I wanted to be back in time before the phone call. *Bring me back, God.* The white was turning black. I was outside my body now as I walked to the end of the docks. *No phone call.* I want the time before. Soon the coldness of the lake with its swirling engulfed me…then nothing but warmth, peace, and a soft white light.

II

POEMS

"If you look for truth
If you look for
Comfort,
You will not
Get neither the comfort
Nor truth, only
Soft sayings and
Wishful thinking
To begin and in the
End despair."

— C. S. Lewis

Meanings of Life

The names on the tombstone
Seem to be
As mysterious as the sounds
Of the wind
Coming off the lake.

———

Today I saw
The clouds both white and dark
Make figures of the Greek gods.
I think maybe when I die
I'll become a cloud
Changing my shape
By the pitch of the wind.

———

The dark grey days
And the black clouds
Eventually bring in
The veil of the night.

———

In the fall as things
Are dying
I know I'll be
Reborn again
Sometime
In the spring.

———

Life must be lived joyfully
Yet despair and melancholy
Find their way in us.

———

Words mean very little.
It's what the heart
Is trying to say
That is important.

———

When will I find someone who
Will talk with me about
The things of the soul and life.
Is there no one?
Where do I find that person?
Perhaps that person is only
Within me and I guess
I must learn to accept
I am an orphan,
But still I need a father
Or God
To help me to put things in
Perspective
Or answer questions of life.

———

If I was anything but
What I am I
Would be nothing.

————

I don't know how much
Longer I can be a fraud,
Saying things I don't mean
And know as soon as I
Say it that I'm lying.
Is there any thing that I say
That I do mean, or is all a lie?

————

I feel so stupid
When I can't answer
Children's questions.
They are eternal questions,
The same we adults ask,
But theirs are more honest.

————

Why as a friend
Sometimes am I not willing
To make a sacrifice
Only willing to take?

————

Some days I don't hear
Anything but that voice inside
Some days I just feel
Like existing and not interacting
With the world.

————

Dream—
God or Devil
Take my soul
Let it be over—every day
One of you takes
Away some part of me.

———

I keep hearing in my dreams
A voice of a
Spanish boy speaking
To his teacher
That "la luz
Brilla para mi—para mi—para mi,"
That "the light does
Shine for me—for me—for me"
Then it fades out.

———

I'm scared to take
That risk that will
Bring me closer to understanding
The relationship of "I" and life.

———

I need to intellectualize and
Talk about nothing—So false
With big words, names, theories,
Concepts, so that actually after I
Finish speaking one has to ask
What is he saying –
Soulless and passionless both in
The writing and in relationships.

———

I feel many times before
I speak the child
Within me
The metamorphosis from
The child to me
Is pulling, growing,
Stumbling
Before articulation.

————

It seems that it has
Been ages since
I had someone to
Talk to about the
Important things of life
I'm waking up to what seems
What was a peaceful sleep
When suicide and
Blowing my brains out
Runs through my mind.

————

Our roles
Are our souls today.

————

I like to see
The whole world order
And in a second
See how it evolved
In different paths of the world
Somehow last night
I think I did see it in
My dreams.

————

Is there another
Me in some other place
I wonder what he
Looks like.

———

I had a glimpse of what
The harmony of life looks like
But it came crashing down
So hard that
I didn't think I
Was going to make it back.

———

I must bring unity
To the different
Aberrations that
Fight each other
In me.

———

What would life be like
Without sex, melancholy, despair
And it is terrible to say
Life is only putting in time
Like a play.

———

I have accepted death
As my ally.
I realize it must
Come and makes no difference
When it does.

———

When a person is sick
He loses the will to live
And death seems for him so
much
Better now in the midst
Of his suffering.

———

Days I cannot
Think or write or talk
Seems like a reprieve
Before I gain
A great thought!

———

A poet no longer can write
Because he feels it has
All been said
By others in more difficult times.

———

How could one
Write about humanity
If one does not love
Humanity?

———

Truth is so elusive
I think it is there
Then it's gone.

———

Yesterday I attempted
To write some
Beautiful thoughts
But it turned
Into a failure
So hard to find
Inner peace while
My physical part
Is in turmoil.

———

Man is orphan
Constantly changing
From fish
To reptile, to mammal
To man to what?

———

Hot baths smooth
The inner parts
Of my soul.

———

She said I should go
To confession
But I can't go
Until my soul
Says so.

———

Tonight I felt I was
Fading into the
Wallpaper of the room.

———

I feel sometimes
In my writing
My self creeping
Through the
Crack in the wall
More complicated in my writing
More so than in my life.

————

Of late this has become the epitome
Of the excitement in my life—
Even though the newness
The smells of delis, bakery
Shops were happy sounds
And brought back memories of the
North End of Boston—It still
Left me empty –
What am I searching for?
In bars, dancers, people's writings,
Readings, on and on
What am I searching for…?

————

When I'm angry I let
Go with the most
Hateful, hurt-felt verbal assaults
Which tears people apart until
They feel like a eunuch and
Their self-image and energy to
Love exists no longer
Why is there so much hate
And mystery in my soul—Is it
My heritage?

————

I think of dying
And how people will
Feel sorry for me.
Thus I must die from
Something like
Cancer, ALS, etc.
At a young age
At the height of my career.
What will people do
After I tell them?

———

I enjoy listening
To conversations
While sitting in
Another room
Like watching a
Play and never
Getting involved
I guess we all
Like being Peeping Toms.

———

Whatever happens
To our shadows?
Do they go to
Those higher lives
Above?

———

There are so many
Forgotten seconds, moments,
Hours, years…
Uneventful days
In short, life.

———

Two ends of a
Continuum of
Reality…the real
And the abstract.
What exists and
How to survive
In the twilight is
The most difficult
Phase of life.

———

Is there a person
Who doesn't need
Physical contact
Like friends and
Lovers?

———

Time is passing,
Especially reaching
For goals
That seem impossible
In the face
Of death.

———

Only living a blind
Existence and looking
For material crutches
But why can't one
See that the symbols
Of prayer, meditation,
Enlightenment get
Us closer to God?

———

Whenever I'm in a
Bookstore, I look and
Search for books
That have such titles
As meaning of life, essence
Of life, and so on,
I rush through the
Pages, searching for
The answers, but
Nothing but the same
Old shit
Everything leaves me
Empty and I'm mad
Because I have been
Ripped off
By my struggling
Soul.

———

I dream of being
A great author, poet,
People looking to
Me for the answers
Show us the way
I really want this
The prophet image
Or do I?

———

Last night I felt
Death lurking
In the background,
Waiting for me
To close my eyes
And not knowing
What morning
Would be like.

———

One has not
Only one sense
Of history
But many
That make up our
Totality.

———

A quandary of not
Wanting to give
All to my family
But saving
Something for myself
This conflict is a
Bitch.

———

What is the relationship in a painting
Of a tree on a lonely mountain
Standing next to
An old wooden shack?

———

I had a dream that I was
Sitting in a class
And the instructor died
And then someone else
Takes over, then I tell
Him that I am the one
Who knows best,
Yet I feel there is
Something on the
Other side of I don't
Know what
I awake then.

———

Exact reproductions
Move us away
From our interpretations
And so-called civilization
Takes over.

———

In a dream, I'm
Walking alone in a
Dark corridor when
I find a door that opens
To a garden of hope,
I find a higher
Level of paradise
Here
Then suddenly the inevitable
Happens
Melancholy and despair
Catch up with me.

———

Plurality is the Father-
God, Holy Ghost
And son Jesus.

———

I can't cope
With rejection
Even though
For years I did the
Same
Over and over again.

———

Prayer means
Something large
Is there
Therefore
I must believe.

———

The Journey and
The Creation is more
Important than
The Project.

———

Enjoyed turning
On the lights
In students' minds.
Giving them
Insights they never had
Before.
I want a standing ovation
At the end of doing
A Great Teach Thing
Yes! Yes! Yes!
I made it work.

———

He is the lamp
His light reaches every
Nook and corner
Of my Darkness
That's why I am alive.

———

Death is taking
Over her body
Slowly but surely
But
She lives
Because she
Has a zest for Life.
Her friends are
All dead but
She cares about
Living, not Dying.
You see
She feeds
Off our
Activities
Then she becomes
Us.
Her Dream
Memories
Are active.
The more
I see her dying
The more
I appreciate living.

———

Sometimes I
Love hiding
From people
So no one
Can control
Me.

———

At twilight, during a lull in my day,
In the stillness of my room, I listened to transmitted sounds,
"The Shadow," "Green Hornet," "Sam Spade,"
And with one twist the visceral odyssey would begin,
Then there were the Saturday mornings sessions
Starting with the howl, "Plunk your magic twanger, Froggy!"
I thought I was riding on an evening star,
Then there were the Sunday evening sessions,
Histrionics and sometimes epigrams abounded,
Anti-intellectual and banal yes, but never boring
When darkness came, lying in bed,
I found comfort and drowsiness in a voice,
Yet it was always exuberant and eloquent.
My only refuge was looking at
A juxtaposition of thousands of electronic dots.
Situation comedies and old movies alike had symmetry for me,
One of few things left now that I had logical consequences.
Since many uncertainties were budding
I always knew what to expect from electronic heroes and heroines.
Their truths were always absolute.
Meditating and thinking about nothingness
While the electronic dots massaged me.
I think very little else could be said
Of this affection for electronic dots,
Except, maybe, Dear God, a passion for fleeing freedom!

———————

Those early morning
Masses I used to serve
As an altar boy at 5:30 a.m.
Present was myself
And the old ladies
Mumbling and banging
Their rosaries against the
Pews.
Quietly the dawn broke through. It was not
The mass I love but the
Feeling of a peaceful
Calm that prevailed in
Church.
These mornings I felt so close to God
Even though our hearts
Were lost to the
Stillness of the church
And there was Father
Crowley mumbling the
Latin as no one really
Listened
Even sometimes as I tasted
The wine that sweet wine
And it tasted more delicious
Because it was forbidden
And also because it was
Not consecrated...those
Times I served I felt I
Was one with a supreme
Power until the
Words and ceremonies
Became meaningless to
Me.

———

Sitting in those pews as a
Child with other children
In my grade headed
By a nun
Reading from those frail
Brown cards with
Latin we didn't understand
Now they're in English
And we still don't
Understand.

———

Many of my most creative thoughts
Come to me in church
Perhaps something
Is trying to give
Me a sign of the importance
Of the creativity and
Fecundity that exist
In the laws of God.

———

I think there is this
Anarchy in me that
Perhaps motivates me
In some part in me
To not to conform.

———

Man is like a burning
Candle.
The inner is burning
And dissolving and spilling
Over to the outside
But eventually it burns out
Man keeps getting closer
And closer to the order
Of things but
Death is the only
Time inside and outside
Become one
Death is his only answer.

————

I find myself greatly
Confused before
An original thought
Evolves—a feeling
Of Chaos is quite
Evident at the
Beginning

————

While talking to
A supposedly mentally
Challenged young boy
He said when
The sun comes up
History starts
And when it goes down
History rests
Perhaps that is the only
History we will see.

————

Alone in church
I look at the flickering
Of vigil lights on the ceilings,
Walls, statues, etc.
I saw the statues
Moving with the flickerings
I sat down in a pew
To pray but really
It was an excuse
So I can think about
Peace, quiet, and
Solitude and its
Relationship to my
Soul—that is my prayer.

———

Eating in a restaurant and
All at once there is an
Eerie moment of
Silence when everyone
Stops talking—like a
Greater power planned it
Then the musical
Conversation starts up again
I often think
Life is like this
Like a rhythmic beat.

———

Nature

There is a lull
In the winter when everything
Seems to have stopped growing;
All time and life for a while get a reprieve
Then it springs back.

————

Music, sea and a burning
Fireplace are the best therapy
For one who has illness
In the soul.

————

Footprints in the snow
Just fill in
And words about the character
Of this person
According to shoe size
If he or she had shoes.

————

Walking in the snow is
Like rubbing two pieces
Of rubber together.

————

In winter
Everything is so
Nice and Crisp
And sexy.

————

Oh how I need
The sea and its cleansing agent!
Oh how I want it
To be part of me.

———

Those white fluffy clouds
Are being lost to the winter
Brewing in the northeast and
The wind and its voice
Are the vanguard of the
Winter storm.

———

There is a definite part
Of man that he has with nature,
And this is especially felt
In the first day of Spring.

———

Freshness of spring
One could
Smell the green,
And the Earth
After a spring rain.

———

The Ghosts of
The buttercups
Dancing in the
Wind saying something.
I just don't know what.

———

Either early morning or late at night
Something about the silence
One finds the aloneness
With the world and nature.

————

Snow—Almost
So smooth I didn't
Want to walk
On it.

————

I hear the rain
Soaking into
The grass.
The rain falling on the eaves
Sounds like a
Thousand dripping faucets.

————

The sea is so infinite and omnipotent
And problems seem so small
The lake gives me a feeling
Of private solitude and
It belongs to you
The sea is too big to belong
Except to humanity.

————

Music of the storm, wind
Rustling of leaves, swirling sounds,
Hounding against the house
The total music of America
With its brooks, city noises,
All in all making a beautiful
Symphony piece.

————

I see a glimpse of the bright
Sky peeking through
An overcast sky as I just
Lay in bed
Daydreaming about the sea
I remember it being green
And wild.

————

Some leaves are left
On the trees in the winter
Still hanging and
Fighting and making
Music with the wind.

————

I smell spring
And its fullness
In the middle of May
Is the zenith of the seasons
There is harmony, unity
And everything seems to
Connect with each other—

————

God, there is
Something in me
And others that bring
Us to bodies of water
Large and small
Accordingly.

———————

The sun, moon, and stars
Are uncivilized
Once we become civilized
We lose our essence
And existence.

———————

I love the wind blowing the
Fall leaves that are like
The solitary voice that only
Speaks to me.

———————

When spring
Is all new
That is when
All life is the finest.

———————

An isolated tree on a
Slope—constantly reminds me
Of what my life has to be.

———————

The grass freshly mowed
Which sometimes smells like horseshit
And so green and so vivid.

————

There is something about
The first leaves
That turn color prematurely
I feel like saying good
For you, you bastards, you're early
Thanks for a glimpse of true beauty.

————

Fall and its smell
Of crisp crumbling leaves,
Remnants of passing
Summer's fragrance.

————

The trees were dark in color
And mournful in form and attitude
Wreathing themselves into sad,
Solemn, and spiritual shapes.

————

Our lives at the
Core are barbaric
And wild like
The stewing sea.

————

Raking and piling
High the freshly
Fallen leaves
Then jumping in
And feeling the
Crushed leaves
Against my face
Along with feeling
The throbbing earth
Underneath.
Piling, jumping
Laughing—
Everything for the
Moment felt
Right with the
World like
Receiving first
Communion for the
First
Time.

———

The stormy, wild
Surf is like
The chaos in my life.

———

Stormy seas
I am attracted to
Because I hate it
But I love it
This is the way
Of my Life
Calm seas
Just give me
A reprieve.

———

Wild winds
Create noisy
Ghosts.

———

Fading embers
Are like glowing
Sunsets.

———

Wild oceans roar
Smoothing my
Angry soul
Over and over the
Waves tumble and
Tumble and are
Addictive like a
Drug.

———

God is like
A little girl twirling
Around and around in
A bright dress.

———

Sand feels
Cool as it curls
On my twisted toes.

———

Boundaries are
Different than walls
Like the ocean and
The shore one
Blends into the other.

———

The sea makes me
Feel at home
Whatever I feel, see,
And hear it.

———

I want to ride
To the moon
And back on
One of its beams.

———

Cold, dark
Dreary days
Means
Come in in
Order to
Come out.

———

God is there
In the thunder
Of the waves in the
Touching of a woman,
In the smell of
Damp earth
In the speed of a boat
Over a glassy
Mirror and
Finally in the
Oneness of water
Sun and earth
Breathing.

———

Flowers, especially
Mums and roses,
Say to me
Everything is okay
With the World.
Their Beauty
Gives me the
Same feeling
When I look
At Monet.

———

Planting and feeling
The fresh earth
Flowing through
My fingers
Means I'm
Connected to
The stuff
I'm made
Of.

————

Happiness is in a
Laugh, hug, smile
And touch
Sitting and enjoying leaves
Falling in a strong
Breeze.

————

In the dark when
My eyes are closed
The light and rays
Seem to be
Shining behind them.
Total peace and calm.

————

There is something about
Fall and night—dark
That my troubles don't
Seem as great
Whereas in the summer
Light, the insanity is
Almost too bright to
Take at times.

———

When you walk the sea
The fringe of its sandy shore
In the wane of the day
Can wash away a tangle
Of cares as a person's
Hands can smooth
Out a snarl of
Knots in a
String.

———

Love

Oh how I
Wanted to be applauded
I wanted to be loved
Loved, loved.

———

She says she is going to do something
And never does
And feel I must constantly
Tell her what to do
To keep her under my control
And to live her life.

———

Walking down the street
And hoping a pretty girl
Would say My God
I can't resist you
I need you.

———

As I look at her
And she at me
We knew in another
Time and circumstance
The fervor of our eyes
Told the story
That we would meet again.

———

Sometimes I see
You sitting and walking
Straight and soldierly
Regal-like, I guess
Sometimes I see
Your soft brown eyes
Wondering
Sometimes I see
Your Oriental face
Blushing
Sometimes I see
You flashing a quick
Uncertain smile.
Sometimes I see
You are as fidgety as
A young puppy
Then sometimes I see
A glimpse
Of innocence
The kind
Children and
Spring flowers
Have
Like a rainbow
Here and a
Beautiful sunset
There
To be totally free
To love, meet
And see and
Become part of
The universe.

———

Passing by her house
Brings back memories of snow,
Telling me about
Fond memories of her
On cold winter nights
In her den on her couch
And then etc.

―――――

What do you expect from me
What do you want from me
How do you want me to act
"I want out—I want out."

―――――

While I walk down the street—
I pray to God that a person in the
Crowd will be the perfect
Lover I've been looking for—I hope
To hell *she* has the answers
To life—
I just
Don't know anymore.

―――――

As we journeyed
To the other
World through
The most
Intimate love
I felt
I was in the fourth dimension.

―――――

Early morn
A woman
In a bright red night
Gown showing her tits
And ass as she
Hunts for seashells.

———

I find I'm
Too gentle
Sometimes
With women
If they had been
Abused they
Treat me the same.

———

Love must
Have violence
And vice versa
Not in sex but
In each other.

———

I'm sitting at a concert
And I'm more interested
In the girl sitting
Next to me
Our arms touched
As she moved
I could hear her
Nylon stockings
Rubbing against
Each other.
All kinds of sensations were sent
Throughout my body
During intermission I
Saw her reading a book
Called *Sex and One*
Throughout the concert we touched and touched
In the dark
Why didn't she speak
She could have been
The one.

———

III
COMMENTARIES

Real Victims Were Ones Left Behind

In flying to New York City in my job as producer for West Virginia Public Theatre, I'm usually struck by how "normal" it all is.

Normally, the night before I tell my grandchildren that their "Poppy" is going to New York on a plane, and I kiss them good-bye.

And little Megan will look at me, with those big brown saucer eyes twinkling, and flash me a smile that turns me into butter as she says, "I love you, Poppy."

Then I pack. Routine, strictly normal, just as I have done a hundred times.

Normally, the next morning, my wife, Mary, takes me to the Morgantown Airport. And we wait for the plane and talk of family matters: the children, grandchildren, my aging parents in Virginia Beach, Va.

And the planes come, and I go, and come back.

All very normal.

But now, I see on the television people, men, women, old, young, some carrying children, with pictures and placards looking for wives, husbands, lovers, friends, grandfathers and grandmothers, grandchildren.

With emotions barely in check, they ask for information—

Just information, normal questions: "Have you seen ... Was she there ... Did he run away in time ... Where are they taking ... Anything?"

Guest Commentary. Dominion Post, *Morgantown, West Virginia,* *23 September 2001: Sunday edition. Reprinted with permission.*

This is not normal.

Deep in my heart, I know, after seeing the wreckage, hearing the roar of steel, glass, plaster, stone crashing down into the streets, watching the soot settle like dirty snow...

They are gone.

How many Megans have lost a Poppy? How many Marys have lost a husband? How many aging parents have lost a child? How many children have lost a father? How many friends, lovers? How many grandfathers, grandmothers will never again melt, like butter, at the smile and kiss of a loving child?

Sure, I know this country of ours will eventually get Osama bin Laden and his fanatical murderers, but that doesn't matter right now. I don't care. I can't. Too much to take in.

I care only for those people with their pictures, their placards, their hopes and their growing awareness that all will never be normal again for them.

I wonder can they ever bounce back from the events of Tuesday, Sept. 11, 2001? Will each time a telephone rings, will they remember the cell phone call from one preparing to die, or will they pick it up and hope to hear a familiar voice say, "I'm fine. It was a mistake..."

Will the calendar, the inevitable media "anniversary" reviews of the day and the year come back to haunt them? Will they ever really know that he's gone...she's not coming home...or will the "why" of it all, the abject wonder, the awareness of the crushing fragility of life, each in the void once occupied by the one lost.

Then there are the stories of so many of the missing having saved or attempted to save others by staying in their offices to help, stepping aside on the stairs, guiding strangers through the terrifying darkness, or trying to overthrow their captors on a doomed hijacked jet?

That's all we have left. Stories. And we take heart in the very sorrow of them simply because it shows again what a magnificent bunch our countrymen and women can be in a time of crisis.

Americans, God bless 'em.

Yet, now, when I hear the commentators and politicians talk of victims, the thousands dead, burned or injured, I think only of the other victims who have been left behind.

All those who mourn are victims.

And we care, deeply, for those who won't hear ever again those simple words, that I cherish more than ever today, "I love you."

So, then, it is for us to do the only thing we can really do in memory of those who have passed. Reach out to someone you care about, to someone you have forgotten to tell lately, "I love you."

Personally, now, I want to go home to see Mary and Megan and the others. And pray for the dead, and the victims who loved them and search for them…. And thank them for reaching out of the darkness to remind me of how precious a few words can sound.

Maybe, just maybe, it will all seem normal again, someday.

It's Critical We Stop Violence
in Our Schools

In light of the recent stabbings at the Franklin Regional High School in Murrysville, Pa., I wonder how many more young, innocent people have to be killed or wounded before we declare a war on school violence.

Here's a brief report card: Columbine High School – 12 killed, 24 injured; Sandy Hook – 27 killed; West Nickel Mines Amish School – 5 killed, 5 injured.

There are, of course, many more that can be listed. But most importantly, how do we stop the killings?

Some experts say we should outlaw guns, knives and all devices that can be considered a weapon. But can we outlaw sick people from finding a way to kill others and themselves?

Since the recent stabbings, the TV and radio talk shows with the help of clinical psychologists are trying to figure out what motivated the stabber.

Similarly, over the years we have attempted to develop a checklist or a profile for shooters. For the most part, it is difficult to do this.

Standard psychological tests or counseling efforts haven't been successful in predicting those students who commit violent acts.

Some studies point out that bullying or mental illness is the cause. The evidence is still not significant enough to say these

Guest Commentary. Dominion Post, *Morgantown, West Virginia, May 2014: Sunday edition. Reprinted with permission.*

are the true causes of school violence.

One thing that we can say for certain: There is no one illness that is common among the perpetrators.

Educators are desperate for answers. So here come the snake-oil salesman selling their cure-all and security plan packages. On the other hand, Dr. Peter Langman, who wrote *Why Kids Kill: Inside the Minds of School Shooters*, suggests more likely violent students are created by a combination of societal issues and the students' background.

Paul Taylor, in his book *The Next Generation*, points out that fewer marriages, more single-parent homes, living digitally and sometimes not being affiliated with any established religion have caused the young to undergo a drastic change from the previous generations.

Additionally, every time I see on TV the young, innocent faces of students who have experienced the horror of school violence, I want to say to them everything is going to be OK, we adults will fix it for you.

First, we must have a dialogue in schools today with students leading the way.

Second, and most importantly, do what airports have been doing since 9/11. Set up security and metal detectors.

Transportation Security Administration agents are annoying, but we feel safer on planes now. The days of open and accessible schools are done.

Beside this, perhaps WVU, being a land grant institution, could lead the way with our College of Education bringing the best of our researchers together to focus on school violence for the state and also the nation.

There is a huge need for solid research in this area.

Finally, we need to teach students and all school personnel the age-old adage to: "Stop, Look, and Listen."

We are at war, and our enemies may be sitting on either side of us in the classrooms or walking in the hallways. Everyone must be on alert to report the most bizarre rumors or gossip.

Our school attackers may be sick psychologically, but also they may be the new terrorists of the 21st century.

They are hurting our most vulnerable of institutions, schools.

Our Human Spirit

The arts teach and put us in touch with the human spirit. And yet the arts are usually pushed aside or cut back by politicians.

Look at what's happening in Michigan where a school district closed its doors in early March for lack of funds. Other school districts, finding themselves in similar straits, are cutting the arts and so-called frills like the school newspaper.

Libraries, art galleries, dance and theatre companies, symphonies are also experiencing severe cut-backs or elimination.

But the saddest part of these cut-backs is what's happening to the poorest areas of our country. Very seldom have the arts been plentiful in these areas and if the arts do exist they are the first to be cut-back during budget crises.

And this is tragic. Everyone in this country should have an opportunity to read great books, see touching plays, and experience a painter's perception of the human condition.

More so, some of the greatest writers and artists have come from the poor. We need them. We need their expressions of the human condition. If their voices are silenced because of some senator's pork barrel study of mud, we lose.

Time after time, I have seen the negative self-concepts of young people become positive through their participation in the arts. However, we must not only give the impoverished youth but all youth an opportunity to write poetry, draw, paint, sing, dance, be in a play.

Guest Commentary. Dominion Post, *Morgantown, West Virginia, 24 April 1993: Sunday edition. Reprinted with permission.*

As human beings, we also become richer when we learn about the customs, traditions, literature and language of all people. No one group should be considered more privileged because they have the money and the louder voices.

Remember, opera, which has an elitist connotation today, was the music and theatre of the people years ago. Mozart's exquisite "Magic Flute" was written as a vaudeville offering for the "commoners."

Theatre evolved out of the need to teach religious doctrine to illiterate peasants in the Middle Ages. Civilization did not really start to evolve until books could be put in the hands of the common people.

The arts like poetry, painting, music, literature, and sculpture, and the crafts are the most democratic of all institutions. Books and painting don't ask the reader or viewer how many designer jeans they have or what car they drive.

The arts are there for all to enjoy. Everyone should have an opportunity to enjoy the sights and sounds of our human condition.

Thinking back, there is no way to describe fully the excitement I felt when at 12 I saw my first musical on stage.

Literally for two hours, I was swept off my feet by Rogers and Hammerstein's "South Pacific." To this day, I still dream of the utopian island Bali Hai where only pure love and happiness exist. Since then, it has become my frame of reference for heaven.

But I also learned something else from this musical.

I learned that people of different colors falling in love had to deal with problems of prejudice, racism and bigotry. In the Broadway classic "West Side Story" we see similar problems.

Beyond the brilliance of Leonard Bernstein's music, the tension, hate and violence that existed between the Puerto Rican and white gangs packed the biggest wallop for me. I learned then and still believe today that violence begets hate whereas tolerance breeds understanding.

The arts also give us a chance to dream and have heroes. I remember going to the Seward Library in Auburn, New York, and reading books about Stan Musial, Mickey Mantle, Babe Ruth, Bob Feller, and so on.

Of course, recent books have talked about their human faults. So what? These books gave me a chance to dream. If Babe Ruth who was abused as a child and orphaned could make it, then a skinny, hawk-nosed Italian kid could make it to the big leagues.

The arts also teach us to think. I believe learning how to think is more basic than the 3Rs and if we don't know how to think, then we are ripe for conditions of tyranny and mechanical lives.

Sometimes, if we're lucky when we read a book, see a film or play, experience an opera, musical, or painting, it will elevate our spiritual side. In a sense, the arts give us a vision of higher things, of a realm beyond our material world.

When the arts are at their best, they instruct.

On Dec. 10, 1950, William Faulkner, in accepting the Nobel Prize for Literature said it best: "I believe that man will not merely endure; he will prevail. He is immortal, not because he alone among creatures has an inexhaustible voice, but because he has a soul, a spirit capable of compassion and sacrifice and endurance.

"The poet's, the writer's, duty is to write about these things. It is the poet's privilege to help humanity endure by lifting the heart, by reminding humanity of the courage and honor and hope and pride and compassion and pity and sacrifice which have been the glory of his past."

There is no doubt in my mind that governmental economic packages, job packages, low interest loan programs, etc., are all wonderful for our external world.

But what will human beings have if their inner spirit is not being nourished?

Courtesy of Sue Amos.

About the Author

Ron Iannone has degrees from St. Bonaventure University and University of Rochester as well as having attained his doctorate from Syracuse University, with post-graduate work at Harvard. He has written several educational books, articles, plays and screenplays. His books are known nationally, especially *School Ain't No Way: Appalachian Consciousness*, a book of poetry: *An Ethnic Connection and Goals Beyond...Reflections of an Italian-American Poet*, and *Alternatives to the Coming Death of Schooling*.

He has received two lifetime achievement awards for his contributions as a writer, educator, poet, artist, and as an outstanding Italian-American in West Virginia. In 2015 he received the West Virginia University's College of Education Human Services Hall of Fame award.

www.ingramcontent.com/pod-product-compliance
Lightning Source LLC
Chambersburg PA
CBHW031836170626
46807CB00004B/1486